RETURN TO FIRST PRINCIPLES

SECOND EDITION

Budd J. Hallberg

authorHOUSE®

AuthorHouse™
1663 Liberty Drive
Bloomington, IN 47403
www.authorhouse.com
Phone: 1-800-839-8640

First edition published by AuthorHouse 10/19/2009
Second edition published by AuthorHouse 11/21/2012

ISBN: 978-1-4772-6460-7 (sc)
ISBN: 978-1-4772-6459-1 (e)

Library of Congress Control Number: 2012915891

In loving memory of my wife and best friend,
Diana

TABLE OF CONTENTS

Appendices

Acknowledgments

This book would have been impossible without the guidance and suggestions of my friends and colleagues in the academic and financial worlds. In particular,

I extend thanks to Robert J. Allison, Ph.D. (Harvard University), Chair of the History Department and Professor of History at Suffolk University and of the Harvard Extension School, for his review of the essay for historical content and relevance.

I am much obliged to Mary Furlong, M.A. (University of Iowa) for her review of the manuscript for political theory application and consequences.

I owe a debt of gratitude to V. Bruce Hirshauer, Ph.D. (Johns Hopkins University) for his review of the set of essays and his valuable insights and criticism.

I am most appreciative to Tom Joyce, Ph.D. (Georgetown University) for his invaluable comments on the essay for thematic integration of justice and philosophical thought. His comments were invaluable.

I am forever grateful to my former Wall Street colleague Scott Wakefield, A.B. (Yale University) for his perceptive comments about the text. He provided the encouragement to clarify and expand those chapters that dealt with the intricate workings of domestic and global financial markets.

> *True friendship is like sound health, the value of it is seldom known until it be lost.*
> -Charles Caleb Colton (1780-1832)

PREFACE

In his book *The Disuniting of America: Reflections on a Multicultural Society* historian Arthur Schlesinger describes the United States as a "multiethnic society" with an "inherent fragility and combustibility."[1] One might conclude that because of the nature of America, the polity must be vigilant to ensure the nation's socioeconomic and political paradigm remains in tact.

Today, America is in the midst of a social meltdown and "a financial crisis the likes of which has not been seen since the Great Depression of the 1930s."[2] The nation's citizenry has lost their moral compass, forgotten their sense of purpose and operate aimlessly. Furthermore, America's political institutions are corrupt. If these problems are not corrected in the near future the country runs the risk of greater economic and political turmoil, violence and possibly the breaking-up of the nation into a confederation.

A "Confederation" is "an alliance of a number of parties or groups, a more or less permanent union of states with some political power vested in a central authority."[3] Political scientist Samuel P. Huntington cautions that "history is a stark reminder that confederations such as the Austro-Hungarian, Ottoman, and Russian empires, normally have not lasted long."[4]

Niccolo Machiavelli wrote in his book *Discourses on Livy* "republics

---

[1] Schlesinger, Jr. Arthur M. *The Disuniting of America: Reflections on a Multicultural Society.* New York: W.W. Norton & Company, 1998, p. 17. Arthur M. Schlesinger, Jr. (1917-2007) was one of the most prominent American historians of the 20th century. He was professor of the Humanities at the Graduate Center of the City University of New York.

[2] Soros, George. *The Crash of 2008 and What It Means.* New York: Public Affairs, 2008, p. 83.

[3] Pearsall, Judy. (ed.). *The Concise Oxford Dictionary.* New York: Oxford University Press, 1999, p. 298.

[4] Huntington, Samuel P. *Who Are We?* New York: Simon & Schuster Paperbacks, 2004, p. 19.

have some goodness in them and that over time that goodness is corrupted." He holds that when this happens, "it is necessary (for the nation) to draw back often toward its beginning." In other words, the country must "Return to First Principles."[5] The need for this is even more apparent today.

Legal expert Emer de Vattel said, "Next to the care of religion, one of the principal duties of a nation relates to justice."[6] He continues with "Confusion, disorder, and despondency, will soon arise in a state, when the citizens are not sure of easily and speedily obtaining justice in all their disputes: without this, the civil virtues will become extinguished, and the society weakened."[7] Newspapers across America are filled with shocking headlines reflecting de Vattel's proposals.

An argument central to this essay is the notion that the *Constitution* is becoming increasingly irrelevant and that laws are being ignored. As a result, the goodness of the United States has become corrupt. The American citizenry must be constantly watchful and remain alert as to signs that the fabric of the nation remains whole and not unravel. Therefore, if the "Republic" is to survive, the nation must return to First Principles - discussed in Chapter Ten of the text.

---

[5] Machiavelli, Niccolo. *Discourses on Livy.* Chicago: The University of Chicago Press, 1996, pp. 209-211. Niccolo Machiavelli (1469-1527) was a Florentine diplomat, dramatist and political thinker.

[6] Haakonssen, Knud. (ed.). *The Law of Nations.* Indianapolis: Liberty Fund, Inc., 2008, p. 185. Emer de Vattel (1714-1767) was a legal expert. His philosophy became foundational to the development of modern law and political theory.

[7] Ibid.

INTRODUCTION

Major worldwide organizations such as the United Nations and World Bank use societal indices to measure the well-being of populations within specific countries. Based on the results of those measurements, nations are compared and ranked. Among the indices, factors used are: 1) divorce, 2) education, 3) infant mortality and 4) crime. According to the United Nation's Human Development Index during 1980, the United States ranked number one. Today "with inequalities considered, the U.S. ranking for well-being drops... to 13th in the world."[8] When compared to other nations during the same period, America's record is a dismal failure.

According to the Center for Disease Control (CDC), in a report dated May 31, 2001, forty-five percent of all first marriages end in divorce.[9] In their report dated October 17, 2007, the CDC reported that forty-three percent of first time marriages had ended in divorce or separation.[10] Based on CDC statistical outcomes, first time marriages in the United States have about a fifty-fifty chance of success.

The Manhattan Institute for Policy Research reports that "using data from the U.S. Department of Education we are able to estimate that ... only 70% of all students in public high schools graduate, and only 32% of all students leave high school qualified to attend four year colleges."[11]

In another study involving America's youth, the organization Family First Aid writes:

> "The United States has the highest rates of teen pregnancy and births in the western industrialized world. Teen

---

[8] marketplace.publicradio.org/display/web/2010.
[9] www.cdc.gov. Advance Data. Number 323. May 31, 2001.
[10] Divorcelawfirms.com.
[11] Manhattan Institute for Policy Research. *Education Working Paper No. 3*. September 2003.

pregnancy costs the United States at least $7 billion annually.

Thirty-four percent of young women become pregnant at least once before they reach the age of 20 – about 820,000 a year. Eight in ten of these teen pregnancies are unintended and 79 percent are to unmarried teens."[12]

"A new report from the Center for Disease Control and National Center for Health Statistics suggests that the nation's high rates of premature births have caused the United States to rank 30th in the world in infant mortality in 2005, the latest year for which international rankings are available, Reuters reports."[13]

The United States has become a corrupt nation. A number of corporate executives and Wall Street financiers have committed crimes harmful to American society and are now serving long sentences in prison. To illustrate, in 2003 Sam Waksal, former CEO of ImClone, pleaded guilty to insider trading and began serving a seven-year sentence. In July 2005 Bernard Ebbers, CEO of WorldCom, was sentenced to 25 years in federal prison for engineering an $11 billion accounting fraud. On October 23, 2006, Jeffrey Skilling, CEO of Enron, was sentenced to 24 years in federal prison for securities and corporate fraud violations which resulted in the largest corporate bankruptcy in U.S. history. On March 12, 2009 Bernard L. Madoff pled guilty to an eleven-count criminal complaint admitting to have defrauded thousands of investors of "$50 billion."[14] This has been reported to be the largest investor fraud ever perpetrated by one individual. The United States Attorney's Office in New York City reported that "United States District Judge Denny Chin sentenced Madoff to serve 150 years in prison."[15] King's College London pointed out that "The United States has the highest prison population rate in the world, some 714 per 100,000 of the national population…."[16]

It is evident that key socioeconomic indicators and recent convictions

---

[12] www.familyfirstaid.org. May 25, 2009.
[13] Robert Wood Johnson Foundation.
[14] Soros, p. 163.
[15] www.usdoj.gov. 8/4/2009
[16] King's College London. *International Center for Prison Studies.* London: King's College London- School of Law, 2009.

of high-profile personalities point to a decadent and corrupt society in America. Today, the United States is mired in a "financial crisis not like the others which have occurred in recent history."[17] The future of America, both as a nation and world leader, is at stake and there is no longer room for political error resulting in harmful unintended consequences. The country is financially broken and it needs to be fixed now.

From the earliest days the American colonies were thought of by many people "as special preserves of virtue and liberty."[18] The Revolutionary War and its aftermath convinced Americans to embrace the idea that the new independent nation should be a *Republic* governed by a written *Constitution*. These tenets are provided for in Article IV. Section. 4. and Article VII. of the *Constitution* of the United States.[19] For over two hundred years, the United States has provided its citizens liberty and economic opportunity unparalleled in human history. Today all of that hangs in the balance. Either the American people decide to take the necessary steps and return to First Principles, or cry *après moi, le deluge* whereby their offspring will run the risk of perishing at the hands of a totalitarian dictator.[20]

Since the earliest of times societies and economies around the world have experienced destabilizing shocks to their systems. Central government intervention was often required to restore equilibrium. For centuries political theorists have made observations and recorded their findings as to how effective governments have been in wrestling with these socioeconomic 'shock' problems.

America is faced with a myriad of severe socioeconomic and political challenges which are draining our resources and weakening the nation. In an effort to identify workable solutions to these critical problems, the text draws upon the writings of a number of philosophers who have gained prominence as political theorists during the last half millennium. The approach is to juxtapose today's occurrences with historical events and arrive at solutions which have a reasonable chance for success.

In his treatise, *Discourses on Livy*, Machiavelli discusses what happens

---

[17] Soros, p. 93.

[18] Bailyn, Bernard. *The Ideological Origins of the American Revolution*. Cambridge: The Belknap Press of Harvard University Press, 1992, p. 84.

[19] Morison, Samuel E., Commager, Henry S. and Leuchtenburg, William E. *A Concise History of the American Republic*. New York: Oxford University Press, 1983, p. 117.

[20] *after me the flood*. Attributed to: King Louis XV of France (1710-1774).

when civil societies become decadent and corrupt. Most important, he talks about how to salvage a society before it completely deteriorates. Machiavelli says when this happens the leaders of a nation must "draw it back often toward its beginning."[21] That is to say, civil societies must return to First Principles.

Machiavelli argues that when a republic is corrupt its society becomes disordered; much like what is happening today in the United States. He recommends that when this occurs, "If (the nation's citizenry) Wishes (their) Republic to Live Long" (the nation) must "Draw Back Often toward Its Beginning" in order for the country to "regain new life and virtue."[22] They must "renew themselves …toward their beginnings."[23] In other words, if the Republic is to survive, it must return to its First Principles.

De Vattel argues that in order to make justice work, nations must have good laws and trustworthy people in high office to see them executed. He held the best laws are useless if they are not observed by the entire body politic. Today, large numbers of America's citizenry in high places, holding positions of power and influence ignore the rule of law and operate outside the judicial system.

First Principles are those tenets which made a country great in the first place. For the United States, these principles include:

- The idea that the *Constitution* be maintained and serve as the legal basis for America's governmental structure.[24]
- The preservation of the union.[25]
- Safeguard liberty of each individual.[26]
- Protection of every citizen's private property.[27]
- An awareness of the dangers associated with political parties.[28]
- Guard against the problems of factions in society.[29]

---

[21] Machiavelli, p. 209.

[22] Ibid.

[23] Ibid, pp. 209 and 212.

[24] Constitutional Convention. Philadelphia. May 25 to September 17, 1787.

[25] Chernow, Ron. *Alexander Hamilton.* New York: Penguin Books, 2004, p. 246.

[26] The Preamble of the United States *Constitution.* Appendix A, p. 198.

[27] Locke, John. *The Second Treatise of Government and A Letter Concerning Toleration.* Mineola: Dover Publications, Inc., 2002, pp. 13-23.

[28] Washington's Farewell Address 1796. Appendix B, p. 199.

[29] Ketcham, Ralph. *James Madison.* Charlottesville: University of Virginia press, 1990, p. 301.

- Vigilance in regard to those who lust for power and aspire to high government office.[30]
- Minimize the influence and corruption of foreign nations.[31]
- Avoid the accumulation of national debt.[32]
- Hold to the notion that 'honesty is the best policy.'[33]
- The will of the majority should prevail.[34]
- The notion that "everyone will have an equal right to the most extensive basic liberties compatible with similar liberty for others."[35]

The text then draws on a number of philosophers and political theorists such as Jeremy Bentham, Thomas Hobbes, Immanuel Kant, John Locke, Thomas Paine and others to provide the reader with some insights as how to deal effectively with many of the critical problems facing America. The socioeconomic, financial and political crisis the United States finds itself in today is not unique. Nations in the past have faced similar problems. History sheds light on how those countries have dealt with comparable issues. It is important to identify workable solutions and avoid costly unintended consequences.

A number of significant political and economic philosophies have developed during the last two centuries. A review of some of these philosophies, or "isms," will put many of the troubles facing America today in a more understandable context.

The text begins with a discussion about the state of the American family. The discourse then examines a number of events which have caused the United States to find itself in a state of decay and corruption.

---

[30] McCullough, David. *John Adams*. New York: Touchstone, 2001, pp. 101-104.

[31] Washington's Farewell Address 1796. Appendix B, p. 199.

[32] Ibid, p. 186.

[33] Parry, Jay A. and Allison, Andrew M. *The Real George Washington*. Malta: National Center for Constitutional Studies. 2009, p. 513.

[34] Thomas Jefferson First Inaugural Address. Appendix C, p. 211.

[35] "John Rawls (1921-2002) was for many years professor of philosophy at Harvard University and is the author of several works in moral and political philosophy. In *A Theory of Justice* Rawls sets forth a hypothetical contract theory in which the bargainers go behind a veil of ignorance in order to devise a set of fundamental agreements that will govern society. No one knows his or her place in society, class position or social status, fortune in the distribution of natural assets and abilities, or even intelligence. Rawls calls this the original position. Each rational person, that is, one who is normally self-interested but who doesn't know his or her place in society, can judge impartially." Pojman, Louis P. and Vaughn, Lewis. *Philosophy: The Quest for Truth*. New York: Oxford University Press, 2012, p. 587.

The discussion then turns to a radical departure in central economic thought which provided an environment for the worst financial crisis since the Great Depression. These conditions such as the breakdown of the nation's banking system and the resulting economic crisis, the worst since the Great Depression, are placing an intolerable strain on the nation's citizenry. If left unchecked, these conditions have a high degree of probability of erupting into a full-blown meltdown resulting in a collapse of American civil society. The book then turns to political theory and examines in great detail those socioeconomic and political theory "isms" which have driven the Western world for nearly 2000 years. Finally, the book explores a number of ways the nation can repair itself, safeguard the American *Constitution* and restore the nation's goodness by returning to its First Principles.

PART I

A Decadent Society

We're all born brave, trusting and greedy, and most of us remain greedy.

-Mignon McLaughlin

The men the American people admire most extravagantly are the most daring liars; the men they detest most violently are those who try to tell them the truth.

-H.L. Mencken

CHAPTER ONE

AMERICA'S SOCIETY HAS TURNED UPSIDE DOWN

*The Universal Declaration of Human Rights describes the
family as the natural and fundamental unit of society.*
-United Nations

A *family* is defined as "a group consisting of two parents and their children living together as a unit."[36] Today, too many American families fail to meet those criteria. Most families fail as a stable social unit. Now, this formless and disorganized condition in which much of the family unit functions is unprecedented.

The United States ranks fifth highest in the world of failed marriages. Only seventy percent of all students in public high schools graduate. The United States has the highest rate of teen pregnancy and births in the Western industrialized world. In 2005, the nation ranked 30th in the world in infant mortality. The family in the United States currently lacks the necessary stability. Among other things, some contributing factors to this condition include: 1) job related geographical mobility, 2) high divorce rate, 3) financial demands and 4) competing family interests. If the Republic is to survive this direction must be reversed; beginning right now.

The family is the epicenter of society. It is foundational to the office and industrial workplace. Families nurture the development of tomorrow's workforce. It molds the character of public service representatives who work in schools and government and serve in the nation's armed forces. A nation that is comprised of a large number of dysfunctional family

---

[36] Pearsall, p. 512.

units leads to dysfunctional workstations. When this happens venerable institutions begin to decay. They end in corporate and government corruption. Civil societies do not endure under these circumstances. Ultimately they perish at the hands of an elitist group and eventually dissolve.

In 1956, William H. Whyte, Jr., wrote a book entitled *The Organization Man*.[37] The text outlined the ideology of America's corporate elite. It described their training and position in the industrial workplace as well as their ambition for a home in suburbia. Whyte said:

> "The organization man sees the organization as his future. He is trained to see continuity between college and the corporation. He has a willingness to be more ready to accept an authority. The goal for eighty percent of college students upon graduation was to join the big corporation. It was here that generous salaries were paid with pension plan and other benefits. Corporations readily administered aptitude, personality and intelligence tests to ensure employee loyalty and conformity. Living in suburbia was the ultimate social achievement. For them, society has in fact been good – very, very good."[38]

In 1962, social critic Vance Packard outlined a number of steps Whyte's 'organization man' should take in order to navigate successfully his way to that coveted corner office – the Executive Suite.[39] In his book *The Pyramid Climbers*, Packard said there are "Four Rules of Behavior for (Corporate) Survival. They are: 1) Be Dedicated, 2) Be Loyal, 3) Be Adaptable ("meaning *They're Asking for* **CREATIVE CONFORMISTS**") and 4) Be Quietly Deferential."[40]

In the text, Packard devoted a chapter entitled *The Wife: Distraction, Detraction, or Asset?* He noted that "New York executive search firms Ward Howell Associates and Boyden Associates both said, before a final

---

[37] William H. Whyte, Jr. (1917-1999) was an American sociologist and journalist.

[38] Whyte, Jr., William H. *The Organization Man.* Garden City: Doubleday Anchor Books, 1956. pp. 4, 7, 10, 21, 69-70, 74-75, 77, 189, 203, 336, 437 and 438.

[39] Vance Packard (1914-1996) was an American author, journalist and social critic.

[40] Packard, Vance. *The Pyramid Climbers.* New York: McGraw-Hill, 1962, pp. 110-118.

decision is made to place an executive with an organization; 'In most cases, we have to see the wife...' They want to see the wife's 'background, college and health.' We're checking her out for 'drinking, talking and emotional stability'.[41] The executive's wife must demonstrate she is "socially gracious and well-spoken, hold her liquor, and show she is a knowledgeable *member of the team,* adept at relating to her husband's inferiors and superiors in the proper fashion."[42] With justification, these business customs and family unit structures came under attack in the early 1960s.

In his book *The Affluent Society,* economist John Kenneth Galbraith examined America in the 1950s.[43] He described the United States as being financially anchored and a period of economic prosperity for most Americans. That said, it was one of the most politically suppressive decades of the 20th century. McCarthyism (the practice of making accusations of disloyalty or treason without proper regard for evidence) muzzled literary and vocal expression.

Movement in the workplace was restrained. For example, the most talented of women had three occupational choices for work outside of the home. They were: secretary, school teacher or nurse. Societal behavior was ironbound and the dress code was expressed in three words – keep in check. By 1960, the nation's citizenry was poised for a "new direction." People of all stripes were ready to open the windows and let in some fresh air.

This book is about some of the people who took the initiative to open those windows. It describes their socioeconomic and political ideology and traces a near half century of effort to take America in that "new direction." The socioeconomic and political agenda of these key actors would come to influence and bring about the most extraordinary socioeconomic and political transformation in America's two hundred year history. Much of the theoretical framework for this new direction originated decades earlier at the Frankfurt School in Frankfurt, Germany. In the early 1960s, two chief actors would come to have a profound

---

[41] Ibid, p. 57.
[42] Ibid, p. 59.
[43] John Kenneth Galbraith (1908-2006) was a Keynesian economist who taught at Harvard for many years.

influence for new direction aimed at America's social landscape. They were Herbert Marcuse and Betty Friedan.[44]

Marcuse "was a radical individualist and Marxist."[45] Combining Marxist and critical theory of the Frankfurt School, Marcuse argued that Whyte's *Organization Man* was a simplistic work which mischaracterized the true conditions of America's corporate elite.[46] Marcuse held there were those (a large segment of the nation's working, blue collar middle class) "whose life is the hell of (Galbraith's) *Affluent Society*," and that "bosses and owners (were) losing their identity as responsible agents."[47] He believed automation to be the greatest catalyst of advanced industrial society and argued that "labor rightly opposes automation."[48] Ironically, a like discussion can be found in Section G of Karl Marx's *The Grundrisse*.[49] Marcuse concludes "that *Socialism* must become reality with the first act of the revolution."[50]

Marcuse's *One-Dimensional Man* was one of the most provocative

---

[44] Herbert Marcuse (1898-1979) had been a 'theorist' at the Frankfurt School. During the 1920s and early 1930s he studied with Martin Heidegger (1889-1976) who had taught philosophy at Freiburg University. (See Craig, Edward. (ed.). *The Shorter Routledge Encyclopedia of Philosophy.* London: Taylor & Francis Group, 2005, pp. 354 and 616). It was here that Marcuse developed and fine-tuned his arguments regarding critical social theory. In 1936, "the National Socialist (in Germany) drove the Institute for Social Research of the Frankfurt School into exile." (See Craig, p. 285). Thereafter, "the Institute affiliated with Columbia University in New York City where Marcuse became associated with that educational organization. (See Marcuse, Herbert. *One-Dimensional Man*. Boston: Beacon Press, 1964, p. xv. Goldberg, Jonah. *Liberal* **FASCISM:** *The Secret History of the* AMERICAN LEFT *from* MUSSOLINI *to the* POLITICS OF MEANING. New York: Doubleday, 2007, p. 227. In 1964, Marcuse published his decades long work – *One-Dimensional Man*.

[45] Marcuse, pp. xxviii and xviii.

[46] Ibid, p. xlix. "Critical theory demonstrates in what ways contemporary society fails to live up to its own claims. The conception of the good life to which each society makes tacit appeal in legitimizing itself will usually not be fully propositionally explicit, so any critical theory will have to begin by extracting a tacit conception of the good life from the beliefs, cultural artifacts and forms of experience present in the society in question. One of the particular difficulties confronting a critical theory of contemporary society is the disappearance of traditional substantive conceptions of the good life that could serve as a basis for internal criticism, and their replacement with the view that modern society needs no legitimation beyond simple reference to its actual efficient functioning, to its 'instrumental' rationality. The ideology of 'instrumental rationality' thus itself becomes a major target for critical theory." (See Craig, p. 157).

[47] Ibid, pp. 23 and 32.

[48] Ibid, pp. 36-37.

[49] Tucker, Robert C. *The Marx-Engels Reader*. New York: W.W. Norton & Company, 1978, pp. 221 and 278-279.

[50] Marcuse, p. 41.

books to be taken up by the emergent New Left in the 1960s.[51] His literary style is Derridian 'deconstruction.' The book's thesis was a damning indictment of Western societies and their centricity toward bureaucratic administration and conformity.[52]

The second key actor who would come to have a profound influence on American society was feminist Betty Friedan.[53] Like Marcuse, Friedan utilized 'deconstruction' as a literary style in writing *The Feminine Mystique*. The book "changed the lives of millions upon millions of women who (Friedan persuaded to jettison) spent empty hours of endless housework and (find) work, and meaning, outside of raising their children and feeding their husbands."[54]

Friedan argued that the American housewife's work included "the drudgery of washing dishes and clothes, diaper-changing, cooking, cleaning, chauffeuring (the kids), shopping and gardening."[55] Women of the era earned nothing for her labor and had to rely on her husband for an allowance.[56] Friedan seemed to borrow from Marxian theory which held that "The wife became the first domestic servant ... who fulfils her duties in the private service of her family."[57] That is to say, Marx held that "The modern individual family is based on the open or disguised domestic enslavement of the woman ..."[58] Logocentric to *The Feminine Mystique* is the notion "that the highest *value* and the only commitment for women is the *fulfillment* of their own femininity."[59] Marx argues the only way that feminine *value* and *fulfillment* can be achieved is for "the individual family unit to be abolished."[60] *The Feminine Mystique* seemed to be scripted in Marxian-Socialist theory and Friedan's conclusions were divisive. According to Friedan, women had two choices: 1) join the ranks of women *elitists* by shunning the roles of housewife and mother and join the emerging army of women in the so-called productive workforce, or

---

[51] Ibid, p. xi. Goldberg, p. 175.

[52] Marcuse, p. xxix.

[53] Betty Friedan (1921-2006) was a feminist and founder of the National Organization of Women (NOW). In 1963, her book entitled *The Feminine Mystique* was first published. In its first three years in print, the Book sold 3 million copies.

[54] Friedan, Betty. *The Feminine Mystique*. New York: W.W. Norton & Company, 1963, x.

[55] Friedan, pp. 239-240 and 243.

[56] Ibid, p. 45.

[57] Tucker, p. 744.

[58] Ibid.

[59] Friedan, p. 43.

[60] Tucker, p. 744. Goldberg, p. 273.

2) remain a second class citizen and stay at home – "dumb, barefoot and pregnant."

Friedan ignored the fact that in 1962 forty percent of the American workforce was comprised of women. She held steadfast to the notion that women of the 20th century had been trapped in a sort of suspended animation thereby living a life of servitude and misery. Friedan was arrogant. Her ideology was divisive. Friedan's lasting influence on American culture has been polarizing.

Marcuse's and Friedan's 'deconstruction' of America's social landscape resulted in the transformation of the family unit and workplace environment in such a way that large numbers of America's kids became casualties. This is evident in one critical area – the United States ranking in the world in education.[61]

The family unit is a vital component in regard to the strength, stability, and growth of America. It is the way in which a child grows and develops that determines the citizen they will grow up to be. If children feel unstable, either emotionally or physically, they may carry these feelings into adulthood. When their family unit is immersed in financial turmoil, such as parental unemployment, children will be at a disadvantage. If they become disadvantaged adults, it will be detrimental to the nation's growth as a whole.

In their book *Families That Work* Janet Gornick and her colleague Marcia Meyers note the challenges facing today's *Dual-Earner-Dual-Carer Society.*[62] They acknowledge how "American families are struggling to resolve tensions arising from new economic and social arrangements in the family."[63] Gornick and Meyers also point out the serious deficiencies in quality Early Childhood Education Centers for kids whose parents

---

[61] The Organization for Economic Cooperation and Development (OECD) released the results of its 2009 PISA (Program for International Student Assessment) test for 15 year-old students in 65 countries. In the Math and Science tests, all participating regions of China outperformed the United States. Of the top 33 nations ranked, in Science, the United States came in 23rd, in Reading, America ranked 17th and in Math, the United States was next to last. She ranked 32nd.

[62] Gornick, Janet C. and Meyers, Marcia K. *Families That Work.* New York: Russell Sage Foundation, 2005, p.91. Janet Gornick is a member of the Baruch College Political Science Department. Marcia Meyers was professor of Social Work and Public Affairs, University of California, Berkeley, 1995.

[63] Ibid, p. 57.

both work.[64] They further note that "all members of society benefit when parents invest more heavily in the 'production' of well-nurtured children ... (which after all) are "tomorrow's productive workers and civic participants."[65] One way to begin repairing today's family unit is to make it financially beneficial to have either a stay-at-home Dad or stay-at-home Mom capability. Financial incentives and "tax benefits" must be devised to encourage such revised family arrangements.

Education and America's Public Schools.

Parents must demand from their local public school systems representation on school curriculum and textbook "selection committees." This will help ensure the textbooks being used are balanced as to form and content. Classroom lectures should be presented objectively. The selection committee must reject textbooks and curricula which promote political correctness. Parental selection committee representation must rotate every three years. This procedure will help ensure a flow of fresh ideas and prevent *cronyism*.

Nearly all public schools have programs involving sex education for children. In some instances this training begins in the first grade at elementary school. In addition to sex education, and beginning in middle school, all public schools should have a mandatory course offering entitled "Parenting." This course, among other things, would teach students the rigors of being a parent. It would explain the responsibilities associated with parenting as well as explaining the extraordinary financial demands that go with the job, which is full-time. The message is clear and simple. Children are a lifetime commitment; parenting is a lifetime commitment.

Public high schools must ensure their curriculum requires a course in "Civics." "The 'civics report card' issued by the U.S. Department of Education for American elementary and high school students at the end of the twentieth century was disappointing." In his book *Bowling Alone* Robert D. Putnam argues "improved civics education in school should be a part of our strategy - not just 'how a bill becomes law,' but 'how can

---

[64] Ibid, pp. 195-196.
[65] Ibid, p. 109.

I participate effectively in the public life of my community'?"[66] All high school graduates should have a fundamental understanding as to how the government of a Republic operates. They should at least know *The PREAMBLE to the CONSTITUION of the* United States.[67] Students should be familiar with The American's Creed.[68] All Americans should be able to sing at least the first stanza of The National Anthem.[69] Every citizen of the United States should be able to recite the Pledge of Allegiance.[70] Tomorrow's citizenry must be equipped to participate effectively in the affairs of their state and local governments.

A Word about Education and Health Care in America.

Health care in America is fractured. The model is designed to treat sick people and not to seek meaningful solutions for incurable diseases. People need to be taught early on in school to have limited expectations from the medical profession. They must understand that it is their responsibility to maintain good health. Beginning in the first grade and continuing through the twelfth grade of high school, the curriculum should include presentations regarding: 1) good nutrition - foods that harm, foods that heal, 2) the unhealthy effects of obesity, 3) the dangers associated with the use of tobacco products and alcohol and 4) the hazards of using illegal drugs. Healthy nations, such as Switzerland and Australia, are productive nations. Their citizenry typically enjoys a high standard of living and quality of life. Healthy nation-building begins in the classroom.[71]

---

[66] Putnam, Robert D. *Bowling Alone.* New York: Simon & Schuster Paperbacks, 2000, p. 405. Robert D. Putnam is a political scientist and professor of public policy at Harvard University.
[67] Appendix A.
[68] Appendix D.
[69] Appendix E.
[70] Appendix F.
[71] Appendix G

The Institute for Social Research of the Frankfurt School
Frankfurt, Germany (ca 1923)

CHAPTER TWO

DECADENCE

*Most human organizations that fall short of their goals
do so not because of stupidity or faulty doctrines, but
because of internal decay and rigidification. They grow
stiff in the joints. They get in a rut. They go to seed.*
                                                    -James Gardner

Indicators of a well-governed Republic are economic stability, political harmony and social order. Today, America's economy mirrors that of the Great Depression of the 1930s. The United States does not enjoy political harmony but rather is embroiled in disharmony and the nation's society is in shambles. If the nation doesn't change direction soon, it runs the risk of losing the Republic.

In 1996, political activist "Ralph Nader wrote to chief executive officers of one hundred of the largest American corporations ... suggesting they open their annual stockholders meeting by reciting the Pledge of Allegiance to the flag of the republic for which it stands."[72] Half of the corporations didn't have the common decency to respond to Nader's letter. A sampling of those who did respond reveals the following: the respondent for "Aetna's CEO called Nader's idea 'contrary to the principles on which our democracy was founded' and Motorola's respondent condemned its 'political and nationalistic overtones'."[73] His suggestion would have received a more positive and respectful response in the decades prior to the 1960s.

---

[72] Huntington, p. 7.
[73] Ibid.

America's business enterprises must be anchored in core values which are designed to avoid corruption. Metaphorically, Fortune 500 corporations and small businesses are the engines that drive the nation's economy. A vast number of towns and cities have come to rely and thrive on these institutions for their financial strength and economic well-being.

When businesses abandon the moral responsibility they have to the communities in which they are located; the seeds of corporate decay have been planted.

A Republic has political harmony when its citizenry actively engages in identifying, selecting and ultimately voting into high public office people of integrity and high moral character, regardless of political philosophy. Should this process be compromised, the government begins to decay.

Associations, clubs and organizations bring together the nation's citizenry which provides for social order. When people disengage from active participation in these institutions they lose power and influence, and the society becomes decadent.

In his text *By Invitation Only* Steven Schier argues that (political) "Parties lie at the heart of democratic politics" and notes that the strength of parties declined since the later part of the nineteenth century.[74] Schier observes "Party mobilization of the public remains in deep decline and voter participation in national elections remains at a seventy-year low."[75] He notes "Many Americans today, looking back on the parties' era, can find much fault with it. Party power limited voter choice and spawned public corruption."[76] Nations with corrupt political systems do not endure.

Americans spend one half of their awake hours in the workplace. Work-related organizations are a vehicle for social camaraderie. Their chief role however is to provide institutional power to act on behalf of the workers they represent.

Putnam notes that "Union Membership in the United States reached a peak of 32.5 percent of (the) Nonagricultural Labor Force in

---

[74] Schier, Steven E. *By Invitation Only.* Pittsburgh: University of Pittsburg Press, 2000, pp. 46-47. Steven Schier is professor of political science at Carlton College.

[75] Ibid, p. 85.

[76] Ibid, p. 65.

the mid-1950s and declined to 14.1 percent in 2000."[77] He points out that "Between 1953 and 1997 the union membership rate declined by 62 percent within manufacturing, by 79 percent within mining, by 78 percent within construction, by 60 percent within transportation, and by 40 percent within the service sector."[78]

In terms of professional affiliations the results are equally dismal. To illustrate, "while the number of registered nurses in America doubled from 1 million in 1977 to 2 million in 1998, membership in the American Nurses Association (ANA) fell from 190,000 to 175,000. In other words, the ANA's 'market share' was cut in half." The "Average Membership Rate in Eight National Professional Associations peaked in 1960. Its current rate is where it was in 1945."[79]

Putnam observes that "... in the 1990s Americans donated a smaller share of (their) personal income than at any other time since the 1940s." He said that "Beginning in 1961 ... philanthropy's share of Americans income has fallen steadily for nearly four decades entirely erasing the postwar gains."[80] Putnam calls the readers attention to the fact that "... membership in the early 1960s found that the PTA had more members than any other secular organization. The percentage of parents nationwide that joined PTA more than doubled between 1945 and 1960. The reversal of six decades of organizational growth ... came with shocking suddenness in 1960. When the decline leveled off in 1980, membership in PTA had returned to the earlier level of 1943."[81] That is to say, decades of substantive increased parent involvement in the public education of their children was eliminated over night.

Formal secular institutions are critical to the sustainability of a Republic. Active engagement in social, civic and professional organizations by all members of society helps contribute to the "dignity of the whole body."[82] Well greased organizations are able to navigate successfully a diachronic socioeconomic and political landscape. This serves the institution's membership effectively and ultimately benefits all of the body politic. The reason this happens is because society's organizations have

---

[77] Putnam, p. 81.
[78] Ibid, p. 82.
[79] Ibid, p. 84.
[80] Ibid, p. 123.
[81] Ibid, pp. 55-56.
[82] Shakespeare, William. *Macbeth*. New York: Barnes & Noble, Inc., 2007, p. 243.

a tendency to complement one another, thereby providing a reciprocal benefit to all.

When institutions *are allowed to decay, it is a first step to societal corruption.*

This action is symbolic of a nation becoming no longer a nation but a bunch of individuals living in the same place. It is a place that is "hoary Deep-a dark illimitable ocean without bound" and a place where "Chaos is the lower of two primal infinities."[83] It is a return to the state of nature.

"Alex de Tocqueville …acknowledged the uniquely democratic claim of individualism and said:

> "a claim and considered feeling which disposes each citizen to isolate himself from the mass of his fellows and withdraw into the circle of family and friends; with this little society formed to his taste, he gladly leaves the greater society to look after itself."[84]

Putnam makes these startling findings:

> "In 1992 three quarters of the U.S. workforce said that 'the breakdown of community' and 'selfishness' were 'serious' or 'extremely serious' problems in America. In 1996 only 8 percent of all Americans said that 'the honesty and integrity of the average American' were improving, as compared with 50 percent of us who thought we were becoming less trustworthy. Those of us who said that people had become less civil over the preceding ten years outnumbered those who thought people had become more civil, 80 percent to 12 percent. In several surveys in 1999 two-thirds of Americans said that America's civic life had weakened in recent years, that social and moral values were higher when they were growing up, and that our society was focused more on the individual than the community. More than 80 percent said there should be

---

[83] Milton, John. *Paradise Lost*. Mineola: Dover Publications, Inc., 2005, pp. 44 and 309.
[84] Putnam, p. 24.

more emphasis on community, even if that put demands on individuals."[85]

America has allowed venerable institutions to fall into decay. This course must be reversed and there is no time to waste. Viable institutions such as workplace unions, civic organizations such as PTA and professional affiliations like the American Nurses Association, the Major League Baseball Association, the Professional Golf Association and the United States Tennis Association are examples of organizations which describe a well-governed Republic. Rather than making laws to limit their power, legislators must begin to rebuild the crumbling social institutions and wait not a day longer. If the nation fails to act, the nation's citizenry can calmly reflect that "in the midst of the sea lies a ruined land" once called the United States of America.[86]

---

[85] Ibid, p. 25.

[86] Alighieri, Dante. *Inferno*. Canto 14. New York: Oxford University Press, 1996, p. 223.

CHAPTER THREE

CORRUPTION

*France fell because there was corruption without
indignation.*

-Romain Rolland (1866-1944)

In ancient Greece, states began to compete with one another for political development. This action resulted in a struggle of factions within the cities and the principle of corruption began to emerge. This caused a "dissociation of small states from one another" and "Greek Morality had made Hellas unfit to form one common state."[87] "An immense power was concentrated in Athens and democracy (was) abolished."[88] "After the fall of Athens, Sparta took upon herself the Hegemony; but misused it selfishly." The "same corruption is introduced-corruption (in) its undisguised form, (a) blank immorality, (with) vulgar selfishness and venality."[89]

Socrates "spent much of his life in the marketplace of Athens questioning and arguing with his contemporaries' philosophical issues such as what are 'justice, self-control and virtue'?"[90] "Virtue" is "behavior showing high moral standards; a quality considered morally good or desirable."[91] "Honesty" is a virtue. Honesty is "free of deceit; truthful and

---

[87] Hegel, Georg Wilhelm Friedrich. *The Philosophy of History.* New York: P.F. Collier & Son, 1900, p. 265.

[88] Ibid, p. 266

[89] Ibid, p. 271.

[90] Pojman, p. 6. Socrates (470-399 B.C.E.) is considered the father of moral philosophy. Plato (427-347 B.C.E.) was a disciple of Socrates and Aristotle's teacher.

[91] Pearsall, p. 1601.

sincere."[92] Honesty builds "trust" and trust "is the firm belief in someone;" it is the "acceptance of the "truth" of a statement without evidence or investigation."[93] When a person tells a "lie" they make "an intentionally false statement." It results in "a situation involving deception" and "presents a false impression."[94] "Honesty" builds trust among people, and then it is a virtue. "Dishonesty" can be identified as a vice. A "vice" is "immoral or wicked behavior." "Criminal activities involving prostitution, pornography, or drugs, a wicked personal characteristic; weaknesses of character are all vices."[95] When people in positions of public trust succumb to habitual lying, society becomes corrupt and soon disappears.

"When a state dissolves ... it ... takes the common name *anarchy*." Here, "democracy degenerates into ochlocracy (mob rule), aristocracy into oligarchy and royalty into tyranny ..."[96] A tyrant is "a private individual who arrogates to himself royal authority without having any right to it." He governs with "violence and without regard for justice and the laws."[97] Machiavelli argues "whether in a corrupt city one can maintain a free state, and replies 'it is very difficult'."[98]

There is much evidence which gives cause for serious concern that the citizens of the United States are in great danger of losing their Republic. This is due in large part because too many citizens are willing to accept weakness of character in the nation's political leaders. Following are a number of illustrations which provide support for this conclusion.

The mass news media has extraordinary power and influence in forming public opinion about critical issues. It also has a way in framing the image of public personalities. The mass news media is an insufferable institution. If they hold a favorable view about a particular individual, they can raise that person's imagery to nearly celebrity status. If they hold an unfavorable view towards someone, they can nearly destroy that person by making *ad hominem* attacks and engaging in character assassination. To illustrate, during the week of June 8, 2009, a major television personality and evening talk-show host remarked that "the fourteen year-old daughter

---

[92] Ibid, p. 681.

[93] Ibid, p. 1540.

[94] Ibid, p. 819.

[95] Ibid, p. 1596.

[96] Rousseau, Jean-Jacques. *On the Social Contract*. Indianapolis: Hackett Publishing Company, 1987, p. 193.

[97] Ibid.

[98] Machiavelli, p. 49.

of one of the state's Governors 'got knocked-up by a professional baseball player' while the two were attending a professional baseball game," or words to that effect.[99] It was supposed to be a joke and drew laughs from the audience – behavior representative of a decadent society.

Governmental corruption and deception have impacted the accounting profession. The Financial Accounting Standards Board (FASB) was designated by the Securities and Exchange Commission (SEC) in 1973 as the organization responsibile for establishing accounting standards for public corporations in the United States. FASB's responsibilities extend to private financial institutions that carry so-called *toxic assets* on their books. It is these very products which ostensibly have caused the financial crisis in the United States banking system.

FASB's rules require all assets carried on a financial firm's balance sheet to be valued daily by a method called *mark-to-the-market*. This requirement provides for a fair valuation of all the firms' assets should some, or all of them, need to be liquidated at a particular point in time. "Mark-to-the-market" is used to value, stocks, bonds, mutual funds, real estate and of course over-the-counter (OTC) derivative and swap products. It is an accounting tool which provides most valuable information to investors and assists them in making sound investment decisions. Mark-to-the-market brings honesty and integrity to a firm's balance sheet.

On April 2, 2009 a column written by Kevin G. Hall appeared in the *Union-Tribune* which reported that "FASB was expected to relax the rules on how banks value assets that investors no longer are willing to purchase."[100] Current regulation requires banks to value assets on their balance sheets at current market price. The article continued by saying that on March 12, 2009 a Congressional hearing was held whereby it was decided that either "FASB would relax mark-to-market rules" or "Congress would impose new rules (to do so) if (FASB) was reluctant."[101]

The column went on to say that critics of the change in mark-to-market rules argue that this procedure would allow banks to "cook their books by hiding bad assets." Well known investment analyst, Ed Yardeni, was quoted as saying 'I fully agree with investors who insist that mark-to-

[99] Letterman, David. *The Late Show*. New York: CBS, June 8, 2009.
[100] Hall, Kevin G. New Rules to Affect Valuation of Toxic Assets. San Diego: *The Union-Tribune*. April 2, 2009.
[101] Ibid.

market is necessary for honest accounting.' The former chief executive of Fannie Mae, Franklin Raines, said that a relaxation of FASB rules would give rise to a 'distortion in the (bank's) balance sheet that nobody can understand.' Finally, David Wyss, chief economist for Standard & Poor said, 'it gives the appearance of sweeping problems under the rug.'[102]

The matter of FASB relaxing its accounting standards for financial firms holding toxic assets on their balance sheets is discussed in Chapter Five of the text. The point here is a reminder of how serious America's financial problems really are. The American people must force Congress to confront these matters of troubled assets on banks' and brokerage firms' balance sheets and take swift action now to remedy the situation.

The appearance of impropriety is nearly equal to the actual happening. "For the generality of men feed on what appears as much as on what is; indeed, many times they are moved more by things that appear than by things that are."[103]

Perception is reality.

On March 2, 2009, insiders of Citigroup purchased over six million shares of common stock at an average price of $1.25 a share. The 52 week low in the stock was 0.97. As of May 12, 2009 the price of the stock was $3.87 a share. That is an increase in value of nearly two hundred percent on the insider's initial investment in just two months.[104]

In February 2009, insiders purchased nearly 50,000 shares of Bank of America stock in prices ranging from $3.78 to $6.21 a share. The 52 week low in the stock was $2.53. On May 12, 2009, the common stock shares were trading at $12.70. That is an increase of over one hundred percent in value to those insiders in just three months.[105]

During the two day period March 2 – March 4, 2009, insiders of GE purchased 330,000 shares of common stock at prices ranging from $6.73 to $8.89 a share. The 52 week low in the stock is $5.73. As of May 12, 2009 the common shares were trading for $13.68 a share. That represents an increase in value between forty and one hundred percent return in just two months.[106] This trading activity by insiders took place during a period

---

[102] Ibid.
[103] Machiavelli, p. 60.
[104] Appendix L.
[105] Appendix K.
[106] Appendix M.

in which the average investor was experiencing severe declines in value of their investment portfolio without much hope for any near term recovery. *Radix malorum est cupiditas.*[107] These transactions and their impact on America's socioeconomic and political landscape are discussed in depth in Chapter Seven

On May 14, 2009 a column appeared in the *New York Times* which reported that the "Governor of New York had called for the resignations of members of the state's ethics oversight commission, hours after 'a report of the state inspector general found there had been a breach of confidential information'."[108] "'This report finds that there has been widespread and continued violation of the public trust' Mr. Paterson, Governor of New York, said Wednesday." "Adding that the report 'indicates that the commission failed to remedy or even recognize these breaches of confidentiality'."[109]

There is strong evidence that corruption has reached crisis levels in nearly all segments of American society. It is found in venerable institutions and at high levels of business and government. People in senior positions of trust and responsibility lie, cheat and steal. They engage in character assassination of their opponents with the most venomous attacks-lampooning their opposition's family including innocent children.

The question often arises, just why do people lie? What is to be gained by lying? Most Americans conclude that the reason people tell lies is out of *fear*. Fear is central to Thomas Hobbes' literary work *Leviathan*.[110] He argues that *man* is in a constant state of war and "in such a Ware, nothing is Unjust."[111] He continues by saying, "The notions of Right and Wrong, Justice and Injustice have there no place." Where there is no common Power, there is no Law: where no Law, no Injustice. The Passions that encline men to Peace are Feare of Death."[112] Most people lie for fear of the consequences of what the truth holds. Today, too many Americans lie

---

[107] Greed is the root of all evil. Chaucer, Geoffrey. *The Canterbury Tales.* New York: Barnes & Noble Classics, 2006, p. 485.

[108] *The New York Times.* Paterson Asks Ethics Panel to Quit After Report Finds Leaks in Spitzer Inquiry. Thursday, May 14, 2009, p. A23.

[109] Ibid.

[110] Thomas Hobbes (1588-1679) "stands out as an innovator in ethics, politics and psychology." (See Craig, p. 371).

[111] Hobbes, Thomas. *Leviathan.* Cambridge: Cambridge University Press, 1991, p. 90.

[112] Ibid.

for selfish advantage just to protect their fiefdom. Lie after lie is symbolic of a decadent society.

Philosopher Immanuel Kant argued that each man and woman must make every effort "of self-denial regarding motives that conflict with the idea of duty and thus with the maxim of striving toward that purity [in one's concept of duty]."[113] Essentially what Kant wanted is for mankind to rise above all the animals and be located just one notch below the angels.[114]

In his book *Common Sense* Thomas Paine argues "the powers of government, may sweep away the liberties of the continent like a deluge."[115] He further holds there are three distinct means of achieving liberty and independence. They are: "By the legal voice of the people in Congress; by a military power; or by a mob."[116] Paine makes this critical observation:

> "The common interest of the community depends on the strength of government, and the happiness of the governed. The inability of *moral virtue* is the design and end of government. That the more simple any thing is, the less liable it is to be disordered, and the easier repaired when disordered."[117]

Paine was a *radical*. His words are a *warning* to those nations which have become corrupt and have lost their bearings to govern effectively. His mode is didactic and he puts forth a conviction that when there is a necessity for a country to return to First Principles it must do so even if it involves great sacrifice.[118]

America's 1980s *Me Generation* has evolved into a society which is characterized by individualism, arrogance and narcissism. The nation has come to embrace an Ayn Rand "philosophy of objectivism, which

---

[113] Kant, Immanuel. *Perpetual Peace and Other Essays.* Indianapolis: Hackett Publishing Company, 1983, p. 68.

[114] Immanuel Kant (1724-1804) "was the paradigmatic philosopher of the European Enlightenment." (See Craig, p. 488).

[115] Paine, Thomas. *Common Sense.* Garden City: Anchor Books, 1973, p. 41.

[116] Ibid, p. 59.

[117] Ibid, p. 15.

[118] Thomas Paine (1737-1809) "immigrated to America in 1774 and settled in Philadelphia where he became a journalist and essayist." (See Craig, p. 764).

advocates a form of ethical egoism, holding that the proper life for rational beings is the pursuit of their happiness and that altruism and self-sacrifice are incompatible with rational morality."[119]

The country has become corrupt and is decadent. These conditions provided an environment which contributed to the financial collapse of America's banking system in the fall of 2008. This event ushered in the worst recession for the United States since the Great Depression of the 1930s. These sociological factors have placed the nation on a perilous road to totalitarianism.

---

[119] "Ayn Rand (1908-1982) wrote several philosophical novels, including *We the Living* (1936), *The Fountainhead* (1943) and *Atlas Shrugged* (1959)." Pojman, pp. 466-467.

PART II

An Economy and Financial System in Trouble

One of the greatest failings of today's executive is his inability to do what he's supposed to do.

-Malcolm Kent

CHAPTER FOUR

A Shift in Economic Philosophy

Banking may well be a career from which no man really recovers.

-John Kenneth Galbraith (1908-2006)

Economic collapse most often "involves the leveraging of debt and real estate, commercial or residential, where the willingness to lend influences the value of the collateral."[120] On December 31, 1930 the New York State superintendent of banking closed the Bank of the United States, a New York City member bank."[121] It was a privately owned financial institution and not a federal government bank as the name miscues. Ostensibly, the "Bank of the United States" had leveraged depositors' funds using mortgages as collateral. When the stock market crashed in the fall of 1929, housing prices also began to tumble; and the "Bank of the United States was ... in pretty poor shape."[122] Shortly thereafter, the decision was made to "let it fail."[123]

The investment banking firm "Lehman Brothers" was founded in 1858. For nearly one hundred and fifty years, the bank had provided investment services to corporate and individual investors. Lehman Brothers became embroiled in credit default swaps and other exotic

---

[120] Soros, p. 59. Yao, Yang and Yueh, Linda. *Globalisation and Economic Growth in China*. London: World Scientific Publishing Co., 2006, pp. 12-13.

[121] Meltzer, Allan H. *A History of the Federal Reserve. Volume 1: 1913-1951*. Chicago: The University of Chicago Press, 2003, p. 323.

[122] Ibid, p. 324.

[123] Ibid. Gordon, John Steele. A Fiasco That Fed the Great Depression. New York: *Barrons*. December 15, 2008.

financial products involving real estate and leverage. In the fall of 2008, "the financial system came close to a breakdown" and the contagion led to Lehman Brothers.[124] Like the Bank of the United States seventy-eight years earlier, the decision was made to "allow Lehman Brothers to fail."[125] Unfortunately, it seems that "what experience and history teach is this, that peoples and governments never have learned anything from history, or acted on principles deduced from it."[126]

The banking system in the United States is the epicenter of *Capitalism*.

Banks create new money by making loans to customers and they circulate money throughout the entire open market system. When banks leverage their portfolios they run a high risk of becoming illiquid. Should banks find themselves in this condition the money supply dries up and in order to remain solvent they begin to call-in loans. This action has an adverse impact on the private sector. In order to remain financially sound, businesses begin to cut costs by laying-off employees. Unemployed workers do not purchase goods and services and the entire economy comes to a standstill. This classic economic cycle typically ends with continued bank failures, a chain of corporate bankruptcies, high and prolonged unemployment, curtailed consumption and a fearful and destitute citizenry. This is the tipping point where capitalism and the Republic are most vulnerable and susceptible to deceptive Marxian political theory-discussed in Chapters Six and Eight of this book.

The numerous bank failures of the early 1930s ushered in the Great Depression. In 1932, Franklin D. Roosevelt (FDR) was elected President of the United States. FDR's arsenal to defeat the Depression was embodied in a program called the "New Deal." The New Deal was bifurcated into sub-programs. The "first" New Deal (1933-1935) was a "top down" economic stimuli approach while the "second" New Deal embraced a "bottom-up" approach. It was this second phase of the New Deal which employed the mechanics and workings of what is commonly referred to as *Keynesian* economics.

In 1936, John Maynard Keynes wrote a book entitled *The General*

---

[124] Soros, p. 161.

[125] Ibid. Paulson, Jr., Henry M. *On the Brink*. New York: Hachette Book Group, 2010, p. 215.

[126] Hegel, p. 6.

Theory of Employment, Interest, and Money.[127] It was here that Keynes "advocated enlightened government intervention over unregulated *laissez-faire* policies."[128] The Keynesian analysis of how monetary and financial arrangements affect the economy "has formed the basis of subsequent activist government fiscal and monetary policy" in the United States.[129]

The question is often asked, what is at the heart of Keynesian economic theory? N. Gregory Mankiw is a professor of economics at Harvard University. He explains it this way. Mankiw says, "In principle, the government can adjust its monetary and fiscal policy in response to waves of optimism and pessimism and, thereby, stabilize the economy."[130]

During the Depression years of the 1930s, many Americans were fearful that Keynesian economics was a *Marxian cover* and would lead the United States in the direction of a Communist dictatorship. There is no evidence Keynes was a Marxist. In fact Keynes argued that Marx "got it wrong" about capitalism and misunderstood David Ricardo's theories regarding economics.[131] In 1817, Ricardo authored a treatise entitled *Principles of Political Economy and Taxation.* His work became foundational to modern-day, market driven, economic theory.

In 1948, Paul Samuelson authored an economics textbook entitled *Economics.*[132] The text has sold over four million copies and for nearly three decades it was the primary economics book used in college and university classrooms nationwide. Samuelson is considered an expert in the field of economics. That said, he "was terribly misguided in his view toward the economic viability of the former Soviet Union," a communist state.[133]

Economist Milton Friedman was critical of Keynesian economic

---

[127] John Maynard Keynes (1883-1946) was a British economist.

[128] Keynes, John Maynard. *The General Theory of Employment, Interest, and Money.* Amherst: Prometheus Books, 1997, p. viii.

[129] Ibid.

[130] Mankiw, N. Gregory. *Principles of Economics.* Mason: Thomson South-Western, 2007, p. 794.

[131] David Ricardo (1772-1823) was an English political economist.

[132] Paul Samuelson (1915-2009) was an American Keynesian economist. Educated at the University of Chicago and Harvard, Samuelson was a professor of economics at the Massachusetts Institute of Technology (MIT).

[133] Taylor, Timothy. Macalester College. *Lecture Seven. The Economy of the Soviet Union.* Chantilly: The Teaching Company, 2008.

theory.[134] In his book *Capitalism and Freedom* Friedman juxtaposed the "welfare state and Keynesian views" and offered a new economic paradigm for America. Friedman's new model would later come to replace Keynesian economic thought. It is called *Libertarian* economic theory. Central to this economic philosophy is the notion that markets do a better job of allocating scarce resources to the citizenry than the government. Friedman argued that for nearly thirty-five years the United States had been wrong when, during the Great Depression of the 1930s, FDR implemented Keynesian economic theory to stabilize the economy. He held that the contemporary economy required a market friendly model more fitting of the times.

Borrowing from The Frankfurt School (discussed in Chapters Six and Seven of the text) and using the tools of *critical theory*, Friedman began to point out how America's Keynesian economic society had "failed to live up to its own claims."[135] Friedman argued the unintended consequences of the "regulation of railroads, the prevailing income tax schedule, monetary reforms, the nation's agriculture and housing program, labor and social security-the record is dismal."[136] Friedman summarized by saying, "Hence the majority of mankind must almost of necessity look with undue favor upon government intervention."[137] This natural bias can be countered only by the existence in a given society "… of a presumption or prejudice in favor of individual liberty, or *laissez-faire*."[138]

Friedman's firebrand form of *laissez-faire* economics, or Libertarianism, would not resonate until the 1980s when, during the Reagan Administration, the idea started to gain traction.[139] It was then, that Friedman's *Libertarian* economic paradigm began to replace the conventional *Keynesian* economic model and became the economic *modus operandi* of the Reagan Administration. President Reagan looked to the marketplace as a domain with "magical powers."[140] Libertarianism's momentum continued through the three administrations which followed Ronald Reagan. They were: 1) Bush the Elder, 2) Bill Clinton and 3)

---

[134] Milton Friedman (1912-2006) was professor of economics at the University of Chicago.

[135] Craig, p. 157. "Tools" of critical theory include: 1) interpretation of the texts, 2) symbolic expressions, 3) critique, 4) criticism and 5) deconstruction – turning the text against itself.

[136] Friedman, pp. 196-197.

[137] Ibid, pp. 197-199.

[138] Ibid, p. 201.

[139] Soros, pp. 93-94.

[140] Ibid, p. 103.

Bush the Younger. Each of these administrations embraced Libertarian economics. In addition to federal administration agendas, Libertarian economics became anchored in academia. It was discussed in a number of advanced textbooks written for college and university classroom presentations.[141]

This shift in economic theory would later come to have profound unintended consequences for America.

In the fall of 2008, a severe economic downturn began and continues to plague America to this day. Its cause can be traced directly to the nation's commercial banking system and their involvement with the trading of highly leveraged real estate swap and derivative instruments. If the United States is to emerge successfully from this debacle, three very basic and fundamental questions need to be asked and answered.

First, during the period 1998 to 2008, what effect did Libertarian economic thought have on federal government policy? Second, in terms of the financial markets, did *Libertarianism* pave the way for the creation and unbridled trading of exotic swap and derivative products? Third, what role did federal regulation, or the lack thereof, have in contributing to the collapse of the nation's economy?

Reflecting on the happenings of the noted ten year period above, the answer is that Libertarian economic theory, the trading of highly leveraged swap and derivative products and passive regulation had a profound impact on the current economic and financial crisis.

In 1998 the Federal Reserve Chairman, Alan Greenspan, testified before Congress. He said:

> "Regulation of derivatives transactions that are privately negotiated by professionals is unnecessary. Regulation that serves no useful purpose hinders the efficiency of markets to enlarge standards of living."[142]

---

[141] Mankiw, pp. 439-442.

[142] The Regulatory Rift That Altered the Debate. Washington: *The Washington Post*. October 15, 2008.

Robert E. Rubin agreed with Greenspan that the "CFTC had no legal authority to regulate derivatives."[143]

Arthur Levitt, Jr., "Like Greenspan and Rubin, (he) questioned CFTC jurisdiction over derivatives and feared a CFTC regulatory effort would cast doubt over the legality of existing derivatives contracts."[144]

The CFTC is a congressionally mandated independent regulatory agency with the responsibility to administer the Commodity Exchange Act of 1936, as amended, which governs the trading of futures and options on futures contracts in the United States.[145] The agency is headquartered in Washington, D.C. Brooksley E. Born was chairwoman of the CFTC during the period 1996-99. She disagreed with Greenspan, Rubin and Levitt regarding the regulation of derivative products. She said, "The size and nature of this (derivative) market create a potential for systemic risk to the nation's financial markets that requires vigilance by federal regulatory authorities."[146] "The warring parties faced off in the Senate Agriculture Committee's hearing room July 30, 1998."[147] Chairman Richard G. Lugar (Republican -Indiana) ... "wanted to extract a public promise from Born to cease her (regulatory) campaign (to have the CFTC gain jurisdiction over the *over-the-counter derivative market*)."[148] Otherwise, Congress would move forward on a Treasury-backed bill to slap a moratorium on further CFTC action. Born had enough. Greenspan, Rubin and Levitt had prevailed.[149]

In "May 1999 Born resigned her position as Chairwoman of the CFTC."[150] The over-the-counter swap and derivative market continued to operate without federal government regulation. This was in large

---

[143] Ibid. Robert E. Rubin was Secretary of the Treasury during the period 1995-1999.

[144] Ibid. Arthur Levitt, Jr., was Chairman of the US Securities and Exchange Commission during the period 1993-2001. The CFTC is an acronym for the U.S. Commodity Futures Trading Commission.

[145] Futures Industry Institute. Guide to U.S. Futures Regulation. Washington, DC: November 1995, p. 1.

[146] The Washington Post. October 15, 2008.

[147] Ibid.

[148] Ibid. In May 2012, Richard E. Mourdock defeated Senator Richard G. Lugar, a six-term incumbent, to be the Republican Party's Senatorial candidate in the November 2012 election. The New York Times. Tea Party Focus Turns to Senate And Shake-Up. Sunday, May 13, 2012, p, 1.

[149] Michael Moore. Capitalism: A Love Story. DVD. Beverly Hills: Paramount Vantage, 2010.

[150] The Washington Post. October 15, 2008.

part the cause of the early 21st century's economic and financial crisis in America.

The Glass-Steagall Act of 1933 was enacted in response to the collapse of America's commercial banking system three years earlier. At the heart of this legislation was a separation of commercial banking activities from investment banking. The purpose of Glass-Steagall was to prevent banks from leveraging their portfolios, provide a risk management capability for investment banking activities and insure customer deposits through the creation of the Federal Deposit Insurance Corporation.

On November 12, 1999 President Bill Clinton signed into law the Gramm-Leach Bliley Act of 1999. This Act repealed the Glass-Steagall Act of 1933.

For all intents and purposes, this action left the commercial and investment banking industry in the United States unregulated. The regulation of the commodity futures markets would undergo massive regulatory reform the following year.

In 2000, the Commodity Futures Modernization Act became law.

That year, Congress repealed a "section of the Act which embodied a public interest requirement that in turn included an economic purpose test (formerly required of new futures contracts before approval for listing on designated commodity exchanges and boards of trade).[151] Without economic purpose, there is no litmus test for commercial usage and application of a *bona fide* hedge transaction. That is to say, if futures contracts are not required to have commercial purpose, they are contrived to do nothing more than provide speculative trading activity and risk management becomes irrelevant. The history and importance of the economic purpose test are well known.

In addition, the *Commodity Futures Modernization Act* removed the prior review and approval process of futures and options on futures contracts performed by the CFTC. These procedures for some futures markets are now vested with the boards of trade and commodity

---

[151] Shilts, Richard. Futures and Binary Options Based on Box Office Receipts. Statement: CFTC, May 19, 2010, p. 4.

exchanges.[152] These actions blur transparency and encourage industry self-dealing. This is contrary to consumer protection and thus flies in the face of the public interest.

For many decades, the economic purpose test and the futures contract approval process enjoyed substantial bipartisan support. These requirements should not only be reinstated under the jurisdiction of the CFTC, these regulations should be strengthened.

The financial collapse of America's banking system which occurred on September 15, 2008 was ten years in the making.

The United States continues to teeter on the edge of bankruptcy. Action needs to be taken in order to restore some sense of stability to the nation's banking system and financial markets. If this is not done, it will be most difficult for the nation to *Return to First Principles* and be governed as a Republic.

The Great Recession of the early 21st century evidences that Libertarianism as an economic theory has proven to be unworkable. It should be abandoned and replaced with the Keynesian theory model. Federal economic policy should embrace a well disciplined, actively monitored and controlled-application of Keynesian economic thought without modification. That means Congress must not abuse the theory as it was originally intended, which they have so often done in the past. For example, Congress should be prohibited from taking funds from deep pocket sources such as the Social Security Fund to support *pork barrel* initiatives. Keynesian economics should be administered as Keynes had outlined in his text. Any member of Congress who advocates economic policy to the contrary is not worthy of the public trust and should not be re-elected to office.

A part of the financial reform law which was approved in July 2010 "sidestepped the 'Volcker rule' (which would ban) banks from short-term trading of securities for their own account and limits investments in private equity groups and hedge funds."[153] "Simon Johnson, professor at MIT, said, 'That's exactly how banks blew themselves up.'"[154] The

---

[152] Economic Requirements Interpretative Statement: Policy Statement on Price Differentials. *U.S. Commodity Futures Trading Commission.* Washington, DC. May 31, 2010.

[153] Guerrera, Francesco, Baer, Justin and Braithwaite, Tom. Wall street set to sidestep 'Volcker rule'. *The Financial Times.* Thursday, November 11, 2010, p. 1.

[154] Ibid.

financial meltdown of Wall Street banks and stock brokerage firms in September 2008 became a global financial contagion. In an attempt to avoid a world depression, international bodies came together to develop a comprehensive set of rules and regulations governing bank and stock brokerage operations. As of March 2012, that effort has failed.

Pablo Triana is a columnist for *The Financial Times*. In an article entitled, <u>Flawed Basel III could boost toxic leverage</u>, he writes "Basel III still contains seeds of more chaos, ... how the bank capital international regulatory framework is, in spite of much-lauded recent modifications, still conducive to leverage-driven crises."[155] He concludes his article by saying, "Basel III would not only permit vast amounts of leverage, but the toxic component of the latter may shoot upwards as banks take advantage of the flawed risk measures sanctioned by policymakers... ."[156]

Several important actions need to be taken for the nation to return to a lasting condition of economic stability.

Congress must reinstate the Glass-Steagall Act of 1933.

This action would separate stock brokerage and commercial banking activities. The result would be to: 1) minimize the use of institutional leverage in conducting financial activities, 2) help safeguard depositors' funds at banks and 3) manage risk inherent in financial markets. This action would sharply curtail the need for future federal government bank and stock brokerage firm bailout.

The Federal Reserve's organizational structure needs to be overhauled.

This is necessary for America to begin the long process of rebuilding its domestic banking and financial system. The new structure must be: 1) based on integrity, 2) grounded in ethical business principles and 3) transparent. This restructuring is essential if America is to recover from its 2008 domestic financial collapse and be able to participate effectively in the global financial markets in future decades.

As a first step, the position of the "Federal Reserve Board Chairman"

---

[155] Triana, Pablo. <u>Flawed Basel III could boost toxic leverage</u>. *The Financial Times*. Monday, November 1, 2010, p. 6.

[156] Ibid. Basel III is a global regulatory framework for banks to maintain certain capital and liquidity Requirements.

must be abolished. That post should be replaced with a newly comprised "Supervisory Board" which would operate much like the Governing Board of the European Central Bank. The reason for this recommendation hinges on the notion that the United States economy and the global financial markets are too vast and complex for one person to manage effectively. In addition, it is highly unlikely that any one individual would singularly possess the skills required to manage the Federal Reserve System in the 21st century. A Supervisory Board's composition would more likely have a collective command of the academic disciplines needed for the many challenges which lie ahead than a single person. Besides, the position of "Fed Chairman" gives way too much *power* to one individual.

America's banking system needs to be restructured.

A majority of banks in the United States are financially sound. They aggressively participate daily in personal and commercial lending activities. A large number of banks continue to be unduly constrained by a handful of large financial institutions whose balance sheets still contain trillions of dollars of worthless paper-namely swap and derivative products. In 2009, that paper was shelved, meaning it was exempt from *mark-to-market* requirements by a direction from Congress (see discussion in Chapter Three). That doesn't mean the paper has disappeared. It means that dealing with the problem has been postponed to sometime in the future. Until the political courage is mustered to deal with this problem effectively; there will be no closure to America's financial crisis.

A two tier banking system needs to be developed.

The two tier banking system would operate as follows: First, banks with sound balance sheets, meaning they do not contain toxic swap and derivative products, would operate on track one without federal government interference. Two, banks with toxic swap and derivative products on their balance sheets, albeit shelved for the moment, would operate on track two with heightened federal government supervision and oversight. Banks on track two would have one year to become solvent. Once they gain integrity, they would be moved to track one. If a bank fails to become solvent within a year's time, they would be permitted to slowly unwind their operation without disruption to the overall market. Depositors would be covered by the Federal Deposit Insurance Corporation during this period. This program should establish 2016 as an end date to accomplish stated goals and objectives.

Over-the-counter (OTC) swap and derivative products should be made unlawful to trade.

The SEC and the CFTC must notify all financial institutions holding OTC swap and derivative instruments on their balance sheets that those positions are for liquidation only and that no new positions may be opened. Once these stale positions are off-set, they should be unlawful to trade. Swaps and derivative products have not proven to be an effective risk management tool for banks, financial institutions, municipalities and corporations. The track record of these products has been dismal (see Chapter Five). There is no general public demand for swap and derivative products. They serve no economic purpose and should be banned from trading in the marketplace.[157]

In order for the United States to emerge from the economic calamity of the early 21st century as a world leader, it is critical the dollar be stabilized in the international currency markets. A first step would be for:

United States debt obligations should be monetized with Gold.

John Maynard Keynes warned "that 'there is no subtler, no surer means of overturning the existing basis of society than to debauch the currency. The process engages all the hidden forces of economic law on the side of destruction.'"[158] The monetary and fiscal policy of the US Treasury and the Federal Reserve under the Obama Administration has done just that

---

[157] When a futures or commodity exchange decides to list a new futures contract, it must first submit the proposed contract to the US Commodity Futures Trading Commission for review and approval. Part of that review process includes economic purpose and public interest. "Under guideline 1 of the Commodities Futures Trading Commission (CFTC), every application by an exchange for a new futures contract must contain a description of the cash market, an analysis of the terms and conditions of the contract, an explanation of how the contract would fulfill an economic purpose, and a statement of how the contract furthers the public interest." Fischel, Daniel R. Regulatory Conflict and Entry Regulation of New Futures Contracts. The Journal of Business, Vol. 59, No.2 (April, 1986), pp. S85-S102. The Commodity Futures Modernization Act of 2000 ended the guideline 1 requirement and ushered in the deregulation of swaps and over-the-counter derivative products.

[158] Klein, Naomi. *The Shock Doctrine*. New York: Henry Holt and Company, 2007, p. 143.

– America's currency is being destroyed and its society is being turned upside down.

It is imperative that a monetization program should begin now with the federal government's long-term Treasury bond being backed by **Gold** and, within two years, extended to include US Treasury Note obligations. Conversion of these two debt instruments would be at par value with a fixed price of Gold at $1,000.00 an ounce. A number of scheduled phases integrating gold into the United States monetary system must be developed. This is essential if lasting confidence in the dollar is to be achieved in world financial and currency markets. It is essential if the nation's society is to remain stable and its' people enjoying peace and prosperity.

The monetization of United States debt offerings with gold will help bring equilibrium to the price of crude oil and stabilize the foreign currency markets. First, the majority of oil producing states monetizes each of their particular currencies with the dollar. A natural arbitrage market will emerge between gold and crude oil thereby bringing calmness to these oftentimes volatile markets. Second, a gold denominated Eurodollar will discourage predatory foreign currency speculation. This will result in a smoothing of the global foreign currency markets. This action will cause an easing of tensions in the monetary and energy world marketplace allowing for nations the time to rebuild their broken banking systems.[159]

To ensure that America continues to operate on sound economic principles and continue to be governed as a Republic, the nation's banking system must be restored to ethic-based business principles. These principles must be grounded in: 1) customer service first, 2) a deep respect for the integrity of the financial marketplace, 3) the notion of guardianship for the institution of banking and 4) the role of fiduciary; holding steadfast to George Putnam's *Prudent Man Rule*. George Putnam, the founder of the Putnam group of mutual funds, articulated his Prudent Man Rule. This rule stemmed from a litigation matter in which his great-great grandfather, Samuel Putnam, presided over in 1830. The matter involved the handling of funds by a trustee. In that decision, Judge Putnam directs trustees:

---

[159] Collier, Paul and Dollar, David. *Globalization, Growth, and Poverty.* Washington, DC: The World Bank, 2002, pp. 69, 71 and 76.

"To observe how men of prudence, discretion and intelligence manage their own affairs, not in regard to speculation, but in regard to the permanent disposition of their funds, considering the probable income, as well as the probable safety of the capital to be invested."[160]

The standard here was foundational to the development of the *Prudent Man Rule*. In essence the Prudent Man Rule directs fiduciaries, when investing on behalf of others, to treat those funds with care as if they were their own.[161]

---

[160] Harvard College *vs.* Armory, 9 Pick. (26 Mass.) 446, 461 (1830).
[161] Edwards, Andrew. Inupiat Eskimos Jump Into PPIP. New York: *The Wall Street Journal*. August 10, 2009.

Adam Smith (1723-1790) was known
as the Father of Modern Economics.

CHAPTER FIVE

The Financial Crisis of the Early 21st Century

Since passage of the Federal Reports Act of 1942, information vital for public regulation of business abuse has been controlled by business itself.
-Mark J. Green

In the early 1980s, the economic model which provided guidance to the nation's industry, financial sector and government for nearly fifty years was replaced with a new economic paradigm. That period was followed by three decades of greed, corruption, cowardice and stupidity on Wall Street and in Washington. That behavior caused a financial crisis in America of major proportions. A series of economic "shocks" and massive financial losses involving the trading of exotic OTC swap and derivative products have caused the United States to spiral into the worst economic disaster since the Great Depression.

This chapter examines the cataclysmic events associated with the September 2008 financial collapse of America's banking system. It begins with an overview of the world OTC swap and derivative market. A number of illustrations are then presented describing the mechanics and workings of the exchange traded futures and options on futures markets to include OTC swap and derivative products. Particular attention should be given to the collapse of Bear Stearns and Lehman Brothers. The call for a moratorium on the *mark-to-market* requirement of swap and derivative products must be re-visited. These events demand the Department of Justice and the Federal Bureau of Investigation to launch massive investigations into various banking and investment firm trading activity leading up to the financial meltdown of Wall Street in the fall of 2008. If those investigations reveal wrongdoing, the Department of Justice must take swift action and prosecute the wrongdoers aggressively. The message must be sent to Wall Street – crime doesn't pay in America.

As of June 2008, the Bank for International Settlements (BIS) estimated the gross market value of OTC derivative and swap contracts to be $20 trillion.[162] The notional amount of these contracts was $684 trillion.[163] For the year 2008, the World Bank reported the world's Gross Domestic Product (GDP) to be $60.1 trillion. [164] The notional amount of OTC swap and derivative products outstanding in 2008 was **ten times** the entire world's GDP. It is the trading of these so-called "toxic products" by major banks and investment brokerage organizations that has put the United States and much of the free world on the brink of monetary collapse.

In April 2009, "Billionaire investor George Soros is quoted as saying on Reuters Financial Television, 'The banking system as a whole is basically insolvent'."[165] Mr. Soros updated his views in an article for the *Financial Times* which appeared on Wednesday, December 15, 2010. The column is entitled <u>Better to rescue banks than states</u>.[166] There he stated, the start of the euro crisis can be traced to 2009 "when the new Greek government announced that its predecessor had cheated and the (nation's) deficit was much larger than reported."[167] He said, the euro, which was "supposed to bring convergence, has produced divergences instead."[168] As a result, imbalances have emerged in both the public and private sectors. Soros went on to say that today, "Policymakers are confronted not only by a currency crisis but also by a banking crisis and a crisis in macroeconomic theory."[169] In other words, there has not been much improvement in the condition of global financial markets since the spring of 2012.

The history of trading OTC swap and derivative products is appalling. In 1994, the Frankfort, Germany based energy and mining company,

---

[162] www.bis.org/statistics/derstats.htm.

[163] Ibid.

[164] www.worldbank.org.

[165] *Barron's*. April 13, 2009.

[166] Soros, George. <u>Better to rescue banks than states</u>. *Financial Times*. Wednesday, December 15, 2010, p. 11.

[167] Ibid.

[168] Ibid.

[169] Ibid.

"Metallgesellschaft lost $1.3 billion trading derivative products. That same year, Proctor and Gamble lost $157 million trading like instruments."[170] On December 6, 1994 Orange County, California claimed bankruptcy after losing $1.6 billion trading in the derivative marketplace. It was the largest municipal bankruptcy in the history of the United States.

In 1995, the centuries-old Barings Bank ceased operations after losing $1.3 billion trading in the OTC derivative and swap market. In 1998, the hedge fund Long-Term Capital Management folded after losing $4.6 billion trading derivative contracts. More recent, the insurance company American International group (AIG) has racked-up over $18 billion in losses trading Credit Default Swaps (CDS). The losses keep mounting and no one takes the initiative to put a stop to this insanity. Given the track record of swap and derivative products and the trading of these esoteric financial instruments by banks and stock brokerage firms, it is clear the OTC derivatives market serves no economic purpose and that it should be shut down. These products are dangerous to global financial stability. To arrive at some explanation as to how the United States banking system has come to edge of destruction, it is important to first have a basic understanding of the mechanics and workings of hedging practices, the role of the speculator in risk management and the regulatory process.

The SEC, the Financial Industry Regulatory Association (FINRA) as well as state governments have regulatory responsibility for the oversight of equity and fixed income markets in the United States. The CFTC has regulatory authority over the trading of futures and options of futures contracts and the designated contract markets on which those contracts are traded."[171]

Some industry definitions may be helpful.[172]

Futures and options on futures contracts are traded on designated contract markets called a Board of Trade. A *Board of Trade* is "any exchange or association, whether incorporated or unincorporated, of persons who are

---

[170] Figlewski, Stephen. *How to Lose Money in Derivatives.* The Journal of Derivatives. Winter 1994. Vol. 2, No. 2. New York: Institutional Investor, Inc., 1994.

[171] U.S. Commodity Futures Trading Commission. *Glossary.* Washington, DC: CFTC Publications, 1992, p. 13.

[172] See *Selected Glossary of Terms*, pp. 199-206.

engaged in the business of buying or selling any commodity or receiving the same for sale or consignment."[173]

A *derivative* is "a financial instrument, traded on or off an exchange, the price of which is directly dependent upon (i.e., 'derived from') the value of one or more underlying securities, equity indices, debt instruments, commodities, other derivative instruments, or any agreed upon pricing index or arrangement (e.g., the movement over time of the Consumer Price Index or freight rates). Derivatives involve the trading of rights or obligations based on the underlying product, but do not directly transfer property. They are used to *hedge* risk or to exchange a floating rate of return for a fixed rate of return."[174]

A *swap* is "in general, the exchange of one asset or liability for a similar asset or liability for the purpose of lengthening or shortening maturities, or raising or lowering coupon rates, to maximize revenue or minimize financing costs. In securities, this may entail selling one issue and buying another. In foreign currency, it may entail buying a currency on the spot market and simultaneously selling it forward. Swaps may also involve exchanging income flows; for example, exchanging the fixed rate coupon stream of a bond for a variable rate payment stream, or vice versa, while swapping the principal component of the bond."[175]

A *speculator* "in commodity futures, (is) an individual who does not hedge, but who trades with the objective of achieving profits through the successful anticipation of price movements."[176]

A *hedger* is a person or entity who takes "a position in a futures market opposite to a position held in the cash market to minimize the risk of financial loss from an adverse price change."[177]

"*Natural hedges*, defined as situations in which aggregate risk can be reduced by derivatives transactions between two parties (called *counterparties*), exist for many commodities, for foreign currencies, for interest rates on securities with different maturities, and even for common stocks where investors want to 'hedge their bets'."[178]

---

[173] Ibid.

[174] Ibid.

[175] Ibid.

[176] Ibid.

[177] Ibid.

[178] Brigham, Eugene F. and Ehrhardt, Michael C. *Financial Management*. Mason: Thomson South-Western, 2008, p. 823.

Trading derivative instruments is a zero sum game.

Unlike the equity and fixed income markets, the trading of futures, options on futures, OTC derivatives and swaps-is a zero sum game. For every "long" (a buy or purchased) position there is a corresponding "short" (a sell or sold) position. For every "buyer" there is a corresponding "seller." For every (dollar) "winner" there is a corresponding (dollar) "loser." Open transactions must be closed-out by the ending contract date. Settlement of futures, options and derivative transaction obligations is consummated either by delivery of the actual commodity or by monetary payment. "The main trade-off between forward (derivative) and futures contracts is design flexibility versus credit and liquidity risks."[179]

How futures, options, swaps and derivatives work.

To illustrate, futures contracts are standardized. Their particular credit risk lies with the Clearinghouse. The liquidity risk associated with futures contracts depends on trading activity; namely the amount of open interest in any given futures contract month. Forward or derivative contracts are not standardized, but rather are customized. Credit risk lies with the individual counterparties and not with a central Clearinghouse. Liquidity risk is embedded with the negotiated exit strategy.

"The goal of a hedge transaction is to create a position that, once added to an investor's portfolio, will offset the price risk of another, more fundamental holding."[180] The word 'offset' is used here rather than 'eliminate' because the hedge transaction attempts to neutralize an exposure that remains on the balance sheet."[181]

Hedging is a form of price insurance. The CFTC describes hedging as "a substitute for a later cash transaction."[182] Henry B. Arthur was an expert on agribusiness.[183] He explains hedging as "successful speculation on the Basis."[184] The most common understanding of the concept of hedging is

---

[179] Reilly, Frank K. and Brown, Keith C. *Investment Analysis and Portfolio Management*. Mason: Thomson South-Western, 2006, p. 852.

[180] Ibid.

[181] Ibid.

[182] CFTC *Glossary*, p. 32.

[183] Henry B. Arthur (1904 -1993) was professor emeritus at the Harvard Business School.

[184] Arthur, Henry B. *Commodity Futures as a Business Management Tool*. Boston: Division of Research, Graduate School of Business, Harvard University, 1971.

simply this; hedging is an equal and opposite transaction in the cash and futures (options on futures, derivatives and swaps) market.

Following are a series of examples which describe the role of the speculator first, and then the hedger-acting in the capacity as risk manager. Illustrations are hypothetical. The thematic in all representations is an anticipated change in interest rates. The instruments used are US Treasury Note futures, options on futures contract(s) and OTC interest rate derivative products. **Note:** The price of US Treasury Notes moves inversely as to the direction of interest rates. For example, if interest rates decline, the prices of treasury securities will rise. If interest rates begin to rise, the price of treasury securities will fall.

A "Hedge Fund" manager believes that interest rates will decline in coming months from the prevailing rate of 4% to 3%. The manager enters into a **speculative** futures position by (buying) or going long one June 2014 US Treasury Notes futures contract with a 4% coupon and one year duration at par, or 100.00. The value of the underlying Treasury Note futures contract is $100,000. Later interest rates decline to 3% as the hedge fund manager forecast. The hedge fund manager decides to realize her trading profit of .98 basis points and closes out the speculative trading position.

Bank A has a portfolio which includes holdings of US Treasury Notes with a face value of $100,000. The maturity of the holding is one year and the coupon interest rate is 4%. The bank's "Fixed Income Portfolio" manager fears that interest rates will begin to rise and is desirous to protect the bank's position against a decline in value. To do so, the banks fixed income portfolio manager decides to hedge the bank's cash position by (selling) or going short, one US Treasury Note futures contract at a price of 100.00. The bank's fixed income portfolio manager's forecast is accurate. Interest rates begin to rise thereby causing erosion in the value of the bank's holdings in US Treasury Notes. Interest rates rose to 5% at which point, the bank's fixed income portfolio manager decided to liquidate the entire cash position and close out the hedge in the futures market. The liquidating transaction reflects a .96 basis point realized loss in the bank's cash market holdings which is off-set by a corresponding .96 basis point profit in the bank's futures market hedge position.

A *"position limit"* is "the maximum position, either net long (purchased) or net short (sold), in one commodity future (or option) or in all futures (or options) of one commodity combined which may be held or controlled by one person as prescribed by an exchange and/or by the CFTC."[185] The purpose of positions limits is to prevent market dominance by any one futures trading participant whether it be a speculator or hedger. Market domination can lead to disorderly markets, manipulation of price movement and a host of other irregularities which can damage permanently the integrity of the contract market. Because of the position limit requirement, when properly used, the derivative market could provide an alternative to those entities using the futures market as a risk management tool.

For example, assume further that Bank A has holdings in US Treasury Notes valued at $200,000 and that it is the bank's policy to hedge their entire risk exposure in the cash market using US Treasury futures contracts. Assume further, that a hedge position limit has been imposed on the bank by the commodity exchange on which US Treasury futures contracts are traded to one contract. **Note:** The reason a commodity exchange would impose such a restriction, is because the exchange would not want a disproportionate number of contracts (a large percentage of the total open interest) held by any one institution. This could cause market disruption, especially during the delivery period when the futures contracts mature. If that were to be the case, this imposition would allow for the bank to hedge only half their position in the futures market and be forced to speculate on the other half of their holdings in the cash market. As an alternative, the bank could approach a *Derivatives-Swap Dealer* and arrange to have them seek a counterparty to assume the risk of the remaining portion of their cash holdings. The swap dealer is successful in locating a Hedge Fund Manager who thinks interest rates will decline and is willing to act as the counterparty to the banks hedge transaction. The Hedge Fund Manager takes the opposite side of the bank's hedge position. In this situation, the bank is now fully hedged. Half of the bank's cash market position (price risk exposure) is hedged in the futures market and the other half is hedged in the OTC derivatives market. The hedge fund is the counterparty to the derivative transaction. Some other futures market participant is the counterparty to the bank's short position in the futures market. Time passes and interest rates do not rise as the bank's Fixed Income Portfolio Manager forecast, but rather declined as the Hedge Fund Manager had predicted. Interest rates declined to 3%

---

[185] CFTC *Glossary*, p. 47.

and the bank's Fixed Income Portfolio Manager decided to close out the entire cash, futures market and OTC derivative market position.

In this illustration, the bank closed out their position in US Treasury Notes with a .98 basis point profit in their cash position, and a corresponding .98 basis point loss in their futures and derivative hedge positions. None of the above illustration reflects transaction costs or *basis* differential. What the examples intend to do is illustrate the mechanics and workings of hedge and speculative trading transactions and the notion of counterparty involvement in futures, options and OTC derivative trading.

The credit bubble was all about leverage.[186]

Both the Great Depression of the 1930s and the Great Recession of the 21st century have been caused by certain banks leveraging their balance sheets and related involvement with real estate investments and their declining values. One feature that makes the Great Recession of the 21st century different and potentially more devastating from the Great Depression of the 1930s is that the current financial crisis has in large part been caused by banks and stock brokerage firms trading lethal investment products commonly referred to as swaps and derivative instruments.

In his Up & Down Wall Street column in Barron's, Alan Abelson said:

> "Wall Street, in its maniacal pursuit of profits, thought nothing of leveraging itself 30- and 40-to-1. In the process, it became a prime agent of the severity of the collapse of not only the markets, but the economy as well- and owes, perhaps, its very existence after the bubble burst to Uncle Sam's generosity."[187]

Tetsuya Ishikawa wrote a book entitled, *How I Caused the Credit Crunch.* He said, "that bankers deserted their clients who had bought mortgage bonds when that market collapsed: 'We had moved on to hurting others in our quest for self-preservation'."[188]

---

[186] Ishikawa, Tetsuya. *How I Caused the Credit Crunch.* London: Icon Books, Ltd., 2009, p. 21.
[187] Abelson, Alan. Send in the Magicians. New York: *Barron's.* June 20, 2011, p. 5.
[188] Ishikawa, p. 7.

Andrew Ross Sorkin is a columnist for the *New York Times*. In his book *Too Big to Fail* Sorkin points out that the goal on Wall Street was to generate commissions and fees for themselves with a reckless disregard for their clients.[189]

Ishikawa and Sorkin describe Wall Street bankers as *Ethical Egoists*. These are people who "always serve (their) own self-interest."[190] That is to say, they "do what will maximize (their) own expected utility or bring about (their) own happiness, even when it means harming others."[191] That is a classic description of *Ethical Egoists*.

Diana C. Robertson is Professor of Legal Studies and Business Ethics at the Wharton School of the University of Pennsylvania. She said;

> "You can take *Ethical Egoism* and you can use it to sanction theft, fraud; possibly even personal assault. A society made up of *Ethical Egoists* would be plagued by opportunistic behavior. The cost of accepting the theory as a legitimate one seems very high."[192]

Americans are now paying the costly price by allowing the nation's commercial and investment banking industry to operate under such a corrupt and flawed theory.

Large numbers of banks, investment brokerage and financial institutions continue to hold trillions of dollars of these OTC swap and derivative products on their balance sheets. There is no viable market for these instruments and for all intents and purposes they are worthless. The banks and brokerage firms involved have not been forced to deal with this problem for fear it may aggravate the ongoing financial crisis of 2008 and propel the economy into a full-fledged Depression. In 2009, Congress and Wall Street cut a deal and agreed jointly to avoid the issue and *shelve* the problem indefinitely.

Susan Pullian and Tom McGinty are columnists for *The Wall Street Journal*. In their article entitled <u>Congress Helped Banks Defang Key Rule</u>, they reported that "Robert Herz, Chief of the Financial Accounting

---

[189] Sorkin, Andrew Ross. *Too Big to Fail*. New York: Penguin Group, 2009, p. 538.

[190] Pojman, p. 460.

[191] Ibid.

[192] Robertson, Ph.D., Diana C. <u>Business Ethics</u>. VHS Format. Philadelphia: The Wharton School of the University of Pennsylvania, 1988.

Standards Board (FASB) was directed by Congressional Representative Paul Kanjorski (D-PA) to 'ease an accounting rule' which required banks to disclose fully their *mark-to-market* valuation of toxic assets carried on their balance sheets."[193] In other words, Congress and Wall Street have postponed the problem of dealing with certain bank and brokerage firm balance sheets which carry large positions of worthless swap and derivative contracts. At some point, federal government officials and Wall Street banking executives are going to have to come to terms with this problem and address the looming crisis *head-on*. Keep this in mind. Like exchange traded futures and options contracts, derivative and swap transactions are a zero sum game. For every trillion dollar losses carried on the balance sheets of certain banks and brokerage firms, somewhere, there is a corresponding profitable position. Those positions and locations must be discovered and identified.

Wall Street continuously tries to 'rip off' the public.

Goldman Sachs is a premier Wall Street investment banking and securities firm. Gary Gensler "was co-head of finance at (that organization) and one of the youngest partners in the history of the firm.[194] In 2008, he was named "to head the Commodity Futures Trading Commission ...."[195] In 2002, Mr. Gensler coauthored a book entitled, *The Great Mutual Fund Trap*. The cover of (the text) shows a faceless banker playing a shell game. Inside, "Mr. Gensler warns investors that Wall Street is continuously trying to rip them off."[196] Wall Street bankers that "rip off the public" may well be breaking the law.

The UK banking commissions "interim report of Sir John Vicker's highlights one thing" and that is the "banking system, on both sides of the Atlantic, is more dangerous now than before the financial crisis began in 2008."[197] The chief difference between now and then, is the widely accepted "too big to fail" theory. Under this scenario, banks are able to

---

[193] Pullian, Susan and McGinty, Tom. Congress Helped Banks Defang Key Rule. *The Wall Street Journal*. Wednesday, June 3, 2009.

[194] Baer, Gregory and Gensler, Gary. *The Great Mutual Fund Trap*. New York: Broadway Books, 2002, p. 336.

[195] *The Economist*. A new sheriff. Washington, DC: September 5th-11th 2009, p. 83.

[196] Ibid.

[197] Boone, Peter and Johnson, Simon. The future of banking: is more regulation needed? London: *Financial Times*. Monday, April 11, 2011, p. 9.

borrow cheaply and make risky bets. If the bank wins on one of those bets, their Executives get to participate financially on the upside. If the risky bet goes sour, taxpayers get saddled with the loss. Based on these conditions, it is not a matter of "if" but rather a matter of "when" the next shoe will drop, and the public will exclaim "here we go again."[198]

Jim McTague is a columnist for Barron's financial publication. In an article entitled Last Word on the Crisis? McTague notes the 'FINAL REPORT OF THE NATIONAL Commission on the Causes of the Financial and Economic Crisis in the United States' "concludes that deregulation precipitated the crisis...."[199] McTague notes that "Among the report's conclusions:

- The business model for Freddie Mac and Fannie Mae as publicly traded, profit-making companies, with government backing and public mission, was fundamentally flawed.
- Goldman Sachs avoided at least a $19 billion loss when the federal government bailed out AIG.
- Enforcement of mortgage regulations by Alan Greenspan's Fed could have prevented the crisis.
- Credit-rating agencies were key enablers of the meltdown."[200]

The Dodd-Frank Wall Street Reform and Consumer Protection Act became effective July 21, 2010. The purpose of this 2,300 page legislation is designed to reign in and regulate, among other financial products, the now, $700 trillion swap and derivative markets. The Dodd-Frank Act is cumbersome and unwieldy. The international swap and derivative market is inextricable and opaque. In all likelihood, this legislation will render itself completely ineffective.

Wall Street and "the City of London" continues to 'rip-off' the public, only this time, it's gotten worse.

Patrick Jenkins in London has written an article for the Financial Times entitled, Banks shift assets to cut pension deficits. The article is absolutely shocking. According to Jenkins, "Some of Britain's biggest banks have

---

[198] Ibid.
[199] McTague, Jim. Last Word on the Crisis? New York: *Barron's*. January 31, 2011, p. 33.
[200] Ibid.

begun quietly ridding themselves of billions of pounds of (worthless) assets they have found difficult to sell following the financial crisis, moving them off their balance sheets and into staff pension funds."[201] The goal of such maneuvering is to remove worthless assets from the bank's own books, and prop-up unfunded, deficit pension portfolios. Jenkins says; "... all the big UK banks are running deficits with insufficient assets to cover projected liabilities."[202] A number of large banks found themselves with portfolios loaded with asset-backed securities tied to the US mortgage market following the September 2008 financial meltdown. Because banks have to mark-to-the-market these assets and pension plans are exempt from such a requirement, this scheme allows the banks to gain from capital and tax relief by making the transaction transfers. Pension Fund managers question the move, expressing concern they are receiving worthless assets instead of cash. This is the most egregious act of bankers imaginable.

If this action becomes epidemic in the United States, it will be the knell of this nation. Simply put, America has compiled a national debt, as of August 3, 2011, of $14.3 trillion. This is a debt ratio of Gross Domestic Product equal to ninety-six percent (96%). If banks and corporations begin to saddle their pension plans with worthless swaps and derivative products, the next generation of Americans will indeed be financially wiped-out, if the United States goes the way of big UK banks. This message has got to be told to the American citizenry and the polity must respond in kind. It is time that Wall Street bankers and Washington legislators stop playing *Three Card Monty* with the nation's well-being. It is a time to *Return to First Principles*.

Congress must direct immediately the CFTC, FBI and SEC to open formal investigations into the trading of OTC swap and derivative financial instruments during the period leading up to and including September 2008. Special emphasis must be given to real estate products- the involvement of Freddie Mac and Fannie May- and positions insured by AIG.

At a minimum, firms to be investigated should include Bear Stearns & Company, Lehman Brothers and insurers of toxic products such as AIG. Analysts assigned to the investigation teams must be required to prepare

---

[201] Jenkins, Patrick. Banks shift assets to cut pension deficits. *Financial Times.* Monday, August 22, 2011, p. 14.
[202] Ibid.

a Trade Practice Analysis (TPA). TPAs are used by litigation consultants and expert witnesses as a tool to: 1) match buy and sell trades, 2) identify parties and counterparties to those trades and 3) trace the money flows. The various TPAs will uncover whether or not banks and brokerage firms were trading opposite customer's positions (self-dealing). The TPA will determine if transactions were *bona fide* hedge or speculative transactions. Most important, the TPAs will discover if any customer's positions were being compromised as a result of the banks and brokerage firm's proprietary trading activities.

Wrongdoers must be prosecuted to the full extent of the law.

Should the outcomes of these various (CFTC, FBI and SEC) investigations reveal wrongdoing in any way by banks and investment brokerage firms, the Department of Justice must take swift legal action and have the wrongdoers prosecuted. The message to future generations of Wall Street executives must be made clear – in America, if you commit a crime, break the law and hurt people financially-you go to jail!

PART III

A BROKEN POLITICAL SYSTEM

Power is what men seek, and any group that gets it will abuse it. It is the same old story.

-Lincoln Steffens

All political parties die at last of swallowing their own lies.

-John Arbuthnot (1667-1735)

The tyranny of legislators is at present, and will be for many years, our most formidable danger. The tyranny of the executive will arise in its turn, but at a more distant period.

-Thomas Jefferson (1743-1826)

CHAPTER SIX

SOCIOECONOMIC AND POLITICAL SYSTEMS

If our economy of freedom fails to distribute wealth as ably as it has created it, the road to dictatorship will be open to any man who can persuasively promise security to all.

-Will and Ariel Durant[203]

A *Republic* is "a state in which supreme power is held by the people and their elected representatives, and which has an elected or nominated president rather than a monarch."[204] A monarchy is "a government by a sovereign head of state, especially a king, queen or emperor."[205] The typical system of monarchy stands in contrast to parliamentarianism where executive power is exercised by groups of free citizens. Modern anti-monarchism can be traced to the overthrow of the English monarchy by the Parliament of England in 1649. This action was followed by the American Revolution of 1776 and the French Revolution of 1792. These two revolutions began the process whereby monarchism as a method of nation governing was abolished by the end of World War II.

A *Constitution* is "a body of fundamental principles or established precedents according to which a state or organization is governed."[206] The United States was founded on Republican ideals to be governed by

---

[203] William James Durant (1885-1981) was an American writer, historian and philosopher. Ariel Durant (1898-1981) was the spouse of William Durant. She co-authored with her husband, *The Story of Civilization*.

[204] Pearsall, p. 1216.

[205] Ibid, p. 918.

[206] Ibid, p. 305.

a Constitution. These two precepts anchored the political framework of early America and were intended not to evolve on a diachronic political landscape. It is argued that should the nation begin to diverge from its *First Principles*, the Republic will fail and *Liberty* will be in jeopardy.

The 'anthropocentric' notion of a Republic enabled the United States "to develop the economic culture of capitalism."[207] The United States readily developed as a capitalist society "in which the means of production-land, labor, and capital were privately owned, available for sale, and devoted to harvesting or making commodities for sale in pursuit of profit."[208]

In 1690, John Locke wrote *The Second Treatise of Government and A Letter Concerning Toleration.*[209] Central to Lockean or "Classical" Liberalism is the notion of the acquisition and governmental protection of private property.[210] Locke's *Liberalism* is associated with the notion of "freedom, toleration, individual rights, constitutional democracy and the rule of law."[211] These concepts were developed during the early stages of the Enlightenment.

In his book *Leviathan* Hobbes "proposes a strong sovereign (monarchy) to impose severe penalties on those who disobey the laws...."[212] In *The Second Treatise* Locke "refuted Hobbesian theories of absolute government in favor of government based on the ultimate sovereignty of the people."[213] For Locke, "all men were by nature 'free, equal and independent,' and were entitled to freedom of thought, freedom of speech, and freedom of worship."[214]

Jeremy Bentham "designed an elaborate system of constitutional law in which representative democracy was a central element."[215] In 1780, Bentham wrote a book entitled, *An Introduction to the Principles of Morals and Legislation.* In that text, Bentham discussed among other things, the

---

[207] Taylor, Alan. *American Colonies.* New York: Penguin Books, 2001, p. 21.

[208] Ibid.

[209] John Locke (1632-1704) "is considered the greatest English philosopher of the modern period." (See Pojman, p. 18). "His work on representative government and human rights greatly influenced the Founding Fathers of the United States." (Ibid). His philosophy of government is **Center** on the "isms" Matrix and called *Liberalism.*

[210] Locke, p. 64.

[211] Craig, p. 570.

[212] Ibid.

[213] Locke, p. iii.

[214] Ibid.

[215] Craig, p. 93.

concept of utility, pain and pleasure, ethics, offenses and punishment.[216] His work developed the historical concept of social responsibility and is called social *Welfarism*. Social *Welfarism* stands just **Left of Center** of *Liberalism*.

Discussed in Chapter Four, Keynes wrote a book entitled *The General Theory of Employment, Interest, and Money*. Keynes advocated for an enlightened government which would intervene over unregulated *laissez-faire* policies.

Keynesian economic theory became the template for economic *Welfarism*. This "ism" stands side-by-side with social Welfarism – both are just **Left of Center** of *Liberalism*.

In his text *The Wealth of Nations* Adam Smith describes in great detail the "capitalistic paradigm" which later became central to the mechanics and workings of commerce in the United States."[217] *Capitalism* stands just **Right of Center** of *Liberalism*.

Ayn Rand championed the notion of objectivism which promotes a form of "ethical egoism" in a person's pursuit of happiness.[218] This philosophy stands in contrast to altruism and self-sacrifice. Rand argues that "altruism and self-sacrifice are incompatible with rational morality."[219] Her philosophy stands **Far Right of Center** of *Liberalism* and is called *social Libertarianism*.

In 1962, Friedman wrote a book entitled *Capitalism and Freedom*. In that text, Friedman outlined a thirteen-point description of what has come to be called *economic Libertarianism*.

Libertarianism is "an extreme *laissez-faire* political philosophy advocating only minimal state intervention in the lives of citizens."[220] It stands **Far Right of Center** of *Liberalism*.

Karl Marx was not a professional philosopher, yet he had completed

---

[216] Bentham, Jeremy. *An Introduction to the Principles of Morals and Legislation*. London: Oxford at the Clarendon Press, 1789. Jeremy Bentham (1748-1832) was an English author, jurist, philosopher and legal reformer.

[217] Smith, Adam. *The Wealth of Nations*. New York: The Modern Library, 2000. Adam Smith (1723-1790) was a "philosopher of public life who constructed a general system of morals which included political economy." (See Craig, p. 962).

[218] Ayn Rand (1908-1982) was a 20th century writer of "several philosophical novels." (See Pojman, p. 466).

[219] Ibid, pp. 466-467.

[220] Pearsall, p. 818.

all requirements for a doctorate degree in philosophy.[221] Marx devoted his life to radical political activity, journalism and theoretical studies in history and political economy."[222] In 1848, Marx and his colleague, Friedrich Engels (1820-1895) wrote *The Communist Manifesto and Other Writings*. At the heart of "Communist" political theory is the "Abolition of private property."[223] Communism stands in direct opposition to Locke's argument regarding the acquisition and protection of private property which defines *Liberalism*. Herein lies one of the most polarizing factors which describe these two chief "isms" and sets the stage for the evolution of various hybrid socioeconomic and political theories which would later be developed.

In the 19th century, the American landscape was dominated by the movement westward and the industrial revolution. During this time, the works of Marx and Engels received little attention. At the turn of the 20th century things began to change. Democracy in America was coming under siege. It was a time when "giant corporations and big businessmen challenged democratic institutions."[224]

According to historian Arthur S. Link the period 1910 to 1917 was "momentous and terrible ..., not only for the American people, but for all mankind."[225] In the United States, 1910 "was the beginning of the disruption of the Republican Party."[226] Four years later (1914) the world would be at war. It was a time when women didn't have the right to vote. Factory workers were becoming increasingly skeptical of the American Dream. Families were gradually being destroyed, rather than fulfilled by the capitalistic-industrial complex.

In 1906, Upton Sinclair wrote his most noted literary work *The Jungle*.[227] It was published by Doubleday of New York City.

The Jungle portrays the meat packing industry as corrupt. It tells of

---

[221] Karl Marx (1818-1883) "was the most important of all theorists of socialism." (See Craig, p. 617).

[222] Ibid.

[223] Marx, Karl and Engels, Friedrich. *The Communist Manifesto and Other Writings*. New York: Barnes & Noble Classics, 2005, p. i.

[224] Croly, Herbert. *The Promise of American Life*. Boston: Northeastern University Press, 1989, p. vii.

[225] Link, Arthur S. *Woodrow Wilson and the Progressive Era*. New York: Harper & Row, 1954, p. xii.

[226] Ibid.

[227] Upton Sinclair (1878-1968) was an early 20th century socialist thinker. He assisted in founding the Intercollegiate Socialist Society in New York City.

the exploitation of immigrant workers.[228] *The Jungle* exposes the packing industry of selling rotten and diseased meat to unsuspecting customers. This action caused a public outcry against the meatpacking industry and helped cause the passage of The Pure Food and Drug Act of 1906.

When a Republic's citizenry becomes anxious over socioeconomic dynamics, the nation becomes susceptible to Totalitarian governance. Within political science, the term totalitarianism has "been used to refer to a distinctively modern form of dictatorship based not only on terror but also on mass support mobilized behind an ideology prescribing radical social change."[229] A number of political systems have been associated with various degrees of totalitarianism. They include: 1) Progressivism, 2) Fascism, 3) Nazism and 4) Communism.

The writings of Herbert D. Croly had a major impact on the former president Theodore Roosevelt."[230] Croly's book *The Promise of American Life* was "the intellectual basis for Roosevelt's (progressive) 'New Nationalism'" which was a socioeconomic and political movement designed to improve the lives of working Americans.[231] Roosevelt and the Republican Party would be unsuccessful in retaining control of the progressive movement. That function would pass to President Woodrow Wilson. Under the Wilson presidency, a comprehensive reform program was enacted into law. The movement associated with these reforms came to be known as *Progressivism*.[232]

The progressive reform program included "stringent regulation

---

[228] "Jurgis could see all the truth now-could see himself, through the whole long course of events, the victim of ravenous vultures that had torn into his vitals and devoured him; of fiends that had racked and tortured him, mocking him, meantime, jeering in his face. Ah, God, the horror of it, the monstrous, hideous, demoniacal wickedness of it! He and his family, helpless women and children, struggling to live, ignorant and defenseless and forlorn as they were-and the enemies that had been lurking for them, crouching upon their trail and thirsting for their blood! That first lying circular, that smooth-tongued slippery agent! That trap of the extra payments, the interest, and all the other charges that they had not the means to pay, and would never have attempted to pay! And then all the tricks of the packers, their masters, the tyrants who ruled them,-the shut-downs and the scarcity of work, the irregular hours and the cruel speeding-up, the lowering of wages, the raising of prices! The mercilessness of nature about them, of heat and cold, rain and snow; the mercilessness of the city, of the country in which they lived, of its laws and customs that they did not understand! All of these things had worked together for the company that had marked them for its prey and was waiting for its chance." *The Jungle*, p. 203.

[229] Craig, p. 1023.

[230] Croly, p. xii. Herbert D. Croly (1869-1920) was a progressive activist and writer.

[231] Ibid.

[232] Link, p. xii.

of industry, woman suffrage, federal child labor legislation, and advanced governmental aid to labor, farmers, tenant farmers, and the unemployed."[233] In essence, the goal of the progressive movement was to use the federal government to reform the economy and advance a social agenda. It helped set the stage for programs associated with the New Deal in the 1930s and the Great Society in the 1960s. *Progressivism* is positioned **Left** of *Welfarism* on the *isms* matrix.

In 1922, Benito Mussolini became the 40th Prime Minister of Italy. In his book, *The Political and Social Doctrine of Fascism*, Mussolini tells of the philosophical basis of *Fascism*. He says, "Fascism is "born for the need for action."[234] Mussolini continues by identifying the problems of the relationships between individual citizens and the state. He discusses the challenges of balancing authority and liberty. Mussolini then juxtaposes political and social will in the context of national interests.[235] He describes Fascism as "believing in holiness and in heroism" and being "an organized, centralized and authoritative democracy" standing in "complete opposition to the doctrines of Liberalism."[236] The foundation of Fascism is the conception of the role of the state. According to Mussolini, the chief duties of the Fascist state include: "1) assure personal safety, 2) guarantee a certain level of well-being and peaceful conditions, 3) educate its citizens, 4) respect and defend religion as one of the deepest spirits of man, 5) oppose a sign of decadence and decay, 6) demand discipline, duty and sacrifice and 7) leave some margin of *Liberty* to the individual."[237]

Fascism's simile with Nazism is that they both view Marxist Socialism, or Communism, as the archfiend.

Mussolini writes:

"The Socialists and Communists, though debating between themselves on doctrinarian questions, vied with one another to show themselves more anti-Fascist than the others. The Communists had no scruples. Every

---

[233] Ibid, p. 54.
[234] Mussolini, Benito. *The Political and Social Doctrine of Fascism*. Mineola: Dover Publications, Inc., 1932, p. 228.
[235] Ibid.
[236] Ibid, p. 233.
[237] Ibid, pp. 237-240.

day they gave proof of their contempt for law, and they evidenced a foolish disregard for the strength of their adversaries."[238]

The notion that there are "family bonds between communism and fascism" is a misguided observation.[239]

In his book *Mein Kampf* Adolph Hitler described the socioeconomic and political theory of *Nazism* which emerged in Germany in 1933.[240] This political ideology was logocentric to the National Socialist German Workers Party. It is associated "with extreme racist or authoritarian views."[241]

Nazism held to "the conviction that the question of the future of the German nation was the question of destroying Marxism."[242] Hitler argued that Marxism "almost invisibly destroyed all the foundations of a healthy conception of economy and state ...."[243] Nazism's economic component embraced the notion that "the task of the state toward capital was ... to make certain that capital remain the handmaiden of the state (for the) preservation of a solvent, national, and independent economy on the one hand, (and) assurance of the social rights of the workers on the other."[244] It held that "faith is often the sole foundation of a moral attitude."[245] The text summarizes Nazism's political theories by saying:

> "Take away from present-day mankind its education-based, religious- dogmatic principles – or, practically speaking, ethical-moral principles – by abolishing this religious education, but without replacing it by an equivalent, and the result will be a grave shock to the foundations of their existence. We may therefore state that not only does man live in order to serve higher ideals, but that, conversely, these higher ideals also provide the premise for his existence. Thus the circle closes."[246]

---

[238] Ibid, p. 99.
[239] Goldberg, p. 177.
[240] Adolph Hitler (1889-1945) was Chancellor of Germany from 1933 to 1945.
[241] Pearsall, p. 952.
[242] Hitler, Adolf. *Mein Kampf*. Boston: Houghton Mifflin Company, 1971, p. 155.
[243] Ibid, p. 156.
[244] Ibid, p. 209.
[245] Ibid, p. 267.
[246] Ibid, pp. 379-380.

Communism is the most extreme of the three socialist political theories. It is comprised of two actions: a revolutionary component and a social restructuring component. Tenets of the revolutionary constituent include abolition of: 1) the family, 2) religion and 3) nationalism. The social restructuring component includes: 1) abolition of the private ownership of all property, 2) a progressive or graduated income tax, 3) abolition of all right of inheritance, 4) confiscation of the property of all emigrants, 5) nationalization of the nation's banking system, 6) place all communications in the hands of the state, 7) state ownership of factories and agriculture, 8) control all aspects of labor, 9) redistribution of the population across the country and 10) education of all children in public schools. In Communist nations, such as the former Soviet Union, liberty is abolished. The Government is in the hands of a Dictator.[247]

Today, as in the past, the goal of Marxist Socialism is to change society radically. Marxist Socialism is characterized by: 1) use of approved language only, 2) indoctrination, 3) groupthink, 4) the development of a loyal following and 5) intimidation and violence. Propaganda is also a core ingredient in this political movement.

Lockean Liberalism is the bedrock of a Republic. It is the epicenter of all socioeconomic and political *isms*. If the United States is to continue to be governed as a Republic and its citizenry's liberty preserved – all Americans must be vigilant and guard vigorously against any intrusion of Totalitarianism into the operation and administration of the state and federal governments. Otherwise, the nation flirts with the threat of tyrannical governance.

---

[247] Marx, pp. 27-28.

CHAPTER SEVEN

THE FOUR VILLAINS

The United States is a Republic, providing the Nation is strong enough to keep it.
-Benjamin Franklin (1706-1790)

Four socioeconomic and political developments, metaphorically the *Four Villains*, have taken the United States to the brink of disaster. They are: 1) political correctness, 2) the American legal system, 3) a warped two party political system and 4) *Duoism* - a totalitarian oligarchy. Two of these four developments must be removed permanently from the American landscape and two must be radically modified.

The situation facing the American people is serious. The United States is in grave danger of losing the Republic. Liberty is at stake for every American. If the nation doesn't take swift corrective action now, the country will very likely become a totalitarian state run by a Marxist styled dictator. It is important for Americans to understand the insidious threat posed by the four villains.

The first villain is *political correctness*. The subject of "political correctness" raises a number of questions. First, what is political correctness? Second, what is its purpose? Other questions also come to mind. What impact has political correctness had on American society? Where did political correctness originate? How did it evolve and come to have such a profound influence on American culture? Finally, in moving forward, what policies should the American people adopt in regard to political correctness?

What is Political Correctness?
And
What is its Purpose?

The original purpose of political correctness was well-intended. It is defined as "the avoidance of forms of expression or action that are perceived to exclude, marginalize, or insult groups of people who are socially disadvantaged or discriminated against."[248] Political correctness was hijacked in the early 1960s and its purpose was transformed to foster a progressive agenda which ensured that social advancements of past decades were permanently secured in American culture.

What impact has Political Correctness had on American culture?

Nancy M. Cavender is professor of English at the College of Marin. Howard Kahane (1937-2010) was professor of philosophy at Baruch College. In their book, *Logic and Contemporary Rhetoric,* they argue that in the past 25 years, a social revolution has taken place in the United States.[249] Cavender and Kahane continue by saying that "this revolution has been mirrored in the linguistics practices of those caught up in it."[250] They go on to say the revolution concerning racial and "gender rhetoric is a part of a larger movement that also has dramatically changed the ways in which we speak ...."[251] The result is that certain locutions have become 'in,' while others are 'out'."[252] Not being aware of what is *in* or *out* can have expensive and ruinous consequences. There is also a legal dimension related to problems involving political correctness.

In recent years, political correctness has been at the forefront of a number of costly lawsuits. In 2009, it was reported that over one million Americans were named in lawsuits which involved political correctness related allegations. Dollar amounts of claims exceeded $1 billion. It has ruined people's reputations permanently and derailed professional careers.

Actions associated with political correctness have been far reaching.

---

[248] Pearsall, p. 1107.
[249] Cavender, Nancy M. and Kahane, Howard. *Logic and Contemporary Rhetoric.* Belmont: CENGAGE, 2010, p. 170.
[250] Ibid.
[251] Ibid, p. 173.
[252] Ibid.

They range from the *silly* to the *awkward* to the *deadly*. Both civilian and military communities have been affected.

The field of education has been fertile ground for politically correct speech. For example in California, the picture of Mount Rushmore has been removed from school textbooks. School officials there have argued that the photograph is offensive to Native Americans.[253] In another instance, "the University of Cincinnati Student Senate has declared their higher institution of learning 'a Columbus-myth-free campus'."[254]

To avoid tension and potential conflicts, many school administrators have banned all displays of religious artifacts and expression during the winter holiday season. Centuries of tradition have been swept away in order to ensure no one is displeased. Specifically, they are fearful of offending children whose parents are atheists. What is interesting, atheists and agnostics represent only 1.6% of the American population. These positions are silly, cowardly and unwise.

The military community has also been affected by political correctness. Ron Smith was a columnist for *The Baltimore Sun*.[255] In one of his articles Smith provided an illustration of how political correctness can lead to awkward situations. Reporting from the United States Naval Academy at Annapolis, Maryland, Smith said "... that Naval Academy leaders removed two midshipmen from a color guard assignment because they were white men."[256] Ostensibly they were replaced by a white female and a black male to display a more accurate representation of the academy's diverse student body.

The Naval Academy's decision to restructure the color guard was the right thing to do – but the way it was handled seems to be lacking a transparent explanation. Naval Academy commandant Captain Matt Klunder; "ordered his brigade commanders to forbid midshipmen from discussing this story with any outsiders."[257] The obvious question that comes to mind is why would he give that order? Why didn't the

---

[253] www.blessedcause.org

[254] Cavender, p. 174. In case you missed it, the point is that Columbus could not possibly have discovered America- Native Americans had lived here for at least 10,000 years before Columbus was born.

[255] Ron Smith died December 19, 2011.

[256] Smith, Ron. Fort Hood massacre shows how political correctness can kill. *The Baltimore Sun.* Friday. November 13, 2009, p. 19.

[257] Ibid.

commandant want the matter discussed in public? One can only speculate that it was because he didn't want the hypocrisy associated with this politically correct action exposed to public scrutiny?

In that same article, which is entitled <u>Fort Hood massacre shows how political correctness can kill</u>, Smith gave a glaring example as to how political correctness helped bring about a deadly and tragic event. In November 2009, Major Nidal Malik Hasan was accused of murdering 13 American soldiers and wounding more than two dozen others at Fort Hood, Texas. On April 18, 2012, a military judge set a new trial date for Hasan.[258]

Major Hasan, a medical officer in the United States Army, is a Muslim. Hasan is said to have displayed an erratic behavior over his military career which often sounded the alarm of trouble ahead. These red flags were ignored by military personnel "for fear of being seen as 'discriminatory' against Muslim soldiers."[259] Army Chief of Staff General George Casey appeared on the news program "Sunday Morning." During that appearance, Casey said, "a greater tragedy than the carnage inflicted on unarmed soldiers by an officer of their own army would be anything that called into question 'diversity' as a priority of the American military."[260] It seems to suggest, Army policy holds that diversity trumps human life.

Where did political correctness originate?

Many Americans will be surprised to learn that some aspects of political correctness can be traced to an old adversary, Karl Marx. He was the chief inspiration for all forms of modern social radicalism. "His life was devoted to radical political activity, journalism and theoretical studies in history and political economy."[261]

Marx argued that language is how revolution is articulated. He went on to say, "... we must invent a new poetry, a new way of writing and thinking about revolution."[262]

---

[258] Fort Hood Press Center.
[259] Ibid.
[260] Ibid.
[261] Craig, p. 617.
[262] Marx, p. xxviii.

The new ways of speaking, writing and thinking which Marx Developed constitute the foundation of political correctness.

The major development in the evolution of political correctness took place not in the United States, but in Germany. At the end of World War I (1918), Germany was a country void of any socioeconomic and political infrastructure. That is to say, the country had practically collapsed.

In the early 1920s, scholars at the Frankfurt School were working on a solution to Germany's problems. Their conclusion was that the answer to the country's troubles was Marxist Socialism, or Communism. It was here, at the Frankfurt School, under the guise of political reform, that political correctness truly came alive.

Political correctness is the morbidity of progressive ideology.

Political correctness is cultural Marxism. It is anchored with power groups. Its effectiveness is measured by how well one group comes to have power over another group within a society. Juxtapose power groups and political ideology, the outcome is often a totalitarian state.

The Institute for Social Research (hereinafter "the Institute"), founded in 1929, was part of the Frankfurt School. Its members were scholars who earlier had conducted social research seeking meaningful solutions to Germany's economic problems. They drew on historical perspective and analyzed "how a rational organization of society might be achieved."[263] Their conclusion was that Germany should adopt Communist Political Theory as the basis for the country's political framework. The National Socialists (Nazis) came to power in 1933. They viewed Communism as the archfiend of National Socialism and shut the Institute down in 1936.

Some researchers and faculty members of the Institute at the Frankfurt School remained in Germany and joined the Nazi party. Others fled into exile. A key actor from the Institute, who would leave Germany and come to have an extraordinary influence on American culture, especially during the social revolution of the 1960s, was Herbert Marcuse. Arriving in the United States in the early 1940s, he became affiliated with Columbia University in New York City.

---

[263] Ibid.

Marcuse was a "radical individualist."[264] Marcuse employed the notion of "negative thinking" (Deconstructive Criticism) and used this literary mode to "engage in a damning indictment of contemporary Western societies...."[265] Marcuse and his works became an inspiration for the "New Left" movement.[266] This movement consisted of a number of radical political groups such as the Chicago Seven, Students for a Democratic Society and Weather Underground Organization – among many others. Central to Marcuse's literary style was the notion of political correctness, a carryover from the Frankfurt School.

In the 1960s, college and university campuses provided the dynamics for socioeconomic and political expression. Borrowing from Marx, they were places of radical social engineering experimentation. Political correctness provided a new way of writing and talking about America's emerging *Great Society* which manifested itself during the social revolution of the mid to late 1960s.

At first blush, political correctness appears innocent and functions only as a facilitator which bridges the gaps among various cultures and allows them to communicate more effectively with one another. However, upon further examination, political correctness reveals itself as a method for a Marxist Socialist government to emerge in the United States; replace the Republic and control the masses. Once this happens, Americans will have traded their liberty for tyranny.

Political correctness is anchored in *otherness*.

It is a most effective tool for certain power groups to exercise control over the majority of America's citizenry. That is to say, *otherness* is anything "other than" the country's cultural and religious majority.

Political correctness plays one power group against the other. This development weakens all groups and causes society to operate continuously in a state of chaos and whirl. It transfers ultimate power to a Marxist Socialist federal government. Peace, prosperity and liberty will be lost. A new consensus is beginning to emerge within America's legal system and academia as to the harm political correctness is having on American society.

---

[264] Marcuse, p. xxviii.
[265] Ibid, p. xi.
[266] Ibid.

Political correctness has become an integral part of America's "Legal System."

Many states have *Speech Code* statutes. Those statutes are the result of speech code theory which provides a paradigm for communication based on societal and cultural factors in a given community. Speech code statutes are regulations which restrict or place limitations upon the freedom of speech. Such codes are common in the private sector, government and universities.

The official purpose of speech codes is to suppress hate speech, combat discrimination and harassment in the workplace and on college campuses. This is a noble purpose. However, as time passed the distinction between speech codes and political correctness blurred. Its earlier purpose became lost and what emerged was a Marxist Socialist form of regulated communication in American society. Political correctness has evolved into a form of coercion affecting freedom of expression.

In 1989, a federal court decision, *Doe vs. University of Michigan,* struck down that university's speech code. The University of Wisconsin developed a speech code policy called "Design for Diversity." In the case *UWM Post vs. Board of Regents of University of Wisconsin,* a student newspaper and several students challenged the university's policy on First Amendment grounds. In 1991, a federal court agreed with the plaintiffs and struck down the policy. "'The Supreme Court has consistently held that statutes punishing speech or conduct solely on the grounds that they are unseemly or offensive are unconstitutionally overbroad,' the court wrote."[267] It is fair to say, that politically correct speech codes that have been challenged in court have not done well.

Colleges and universities are places of ideas. The campus is a place of learning where both sides of socioeconomic and political theories should be able to be debated openly without restriction. The Foundation for Individual Rights in Education is a Philadelphia-based civil liberties group.[268] It condemns speech codes, supports free expression on college campuses, fights for academic freedom and challenges politically correct speech codes by filing court actions. Local, state and federal governments promulgate regulation to foster peace and prosperity among its citizenry. However, politically correct speech codes often reflect government

---

[267] Hudson, David L. hate speech & campus speech codes. firstamendmentcenter.org.
[268] www.thefire.org.

officials' fear of retaliation by minority power groups within the body politic.

Cavender and Kahane argue that political correctness dampens healthy discussions about pressing socioeconomic and political issues facing the United States today.[269] They continue by saying that political correctness most often results in "overtolerance of, even blindness to, the defects and foibles of our own group." which compromises American culture.[270]

In moving forward, what should America's policy be toward political correctness?

Students must be taught responsible speech not hypocritical, politically correct, speech. They should be instructed in the use of polite speech. In other words, students need to be taught how to speak with courtesy to one another and not engage in sanctimonious politically correct speech. This should begin in kindergarten and continue throughout the undergraduate experience.

All public schools, to include state funded colleges and universities, must be required to draft a Code of Ethics. Among other things, that "Code" would mandate that teachers abandon all use of superficial political correctness. In its place, students would be instructed how to engage in *responsible* and *polite speech*. This is in keeping with the original purpose of political correctness. This is important, because "What students are taught in schools affects the way they will thereafter see and treat other Americans."[271]

The United States is becoming increasingly an ideological country. Official policy is enforced by the power of the state.

Anyone who dissents from *Political Correctness* risks losing one's reputation, job or both.

This was the same set of circumstances which occurred in Fascist Italy and Nazi Germany during the 1930s and 1940s. It happens today in the People's Republic of China and North Korea. This development is now on the front doorstep of the United States.

---

[269] Cavender, p. 126.
[270] Ibid, p. 127.
[271] Schlesinger, p. 22.

Jonah Goldberg is a columnist for *The Los Angles Times*. In his book, *Liberal* **FASCISM:** *The Secret History of the AMERICAN LEFT from MUSSOLINI to the POLITICS OF MEANING*, he argues that political correctness "govern(s) through *fear*."[272] Political correctness is "Totalitarian" in nature and rooted in cultural Marxism. If the United States is to remain a Republic as provided for in *The CONSTITUTION of the* United States of America, it is critical that political correctness be removed from the nation's societal landscape.[273]

Too often Americans joke about political correctness. They don't take it seriously. Cavender and Kahane argue that political correctness is part of a revolution. History reminds us that revolutions often have unpleasant and long lasting consequences. Americans must take political correctness very seriously. If political correctness is ignored, the American way of life will be changed permanently. Evidence suggests that the citizenry's liberty is at risk. If left unchecked, the body politic could become nothing more than robots of a Marxist Socialist state.

The second villain is America's *legal system*. The nation's legal system is comprised of state and federal government legislatures, the judiciary and the myriad of lawyers who comprise the American Bar Association.

The First Continental Congress convened in Philadelphia in 1774. Fifty-four delegates were in attendance. Of those present, "nearly half were lawyers and most had received a college education."[274] From the earliest days of the Republic, the United States has been anchored in America's legal system.

In his text *A Theory of Justice* John Rawls posits by saying "I now wish to consider rights of the person as these are protected by the principle of the rule of law."[275] To better craft his arguments, Rawls looks back to Immanuel Kant and Kant's "interpretation of *justice as fairness*."[276]

---

[272] Goldberg, p. 282.

[273] The CONSTITUTION *of the* United States of America. Article. IV. Section. 4.

[274] McCullough, p. 85.

[275] Rawls, John. *A Theory of Justice*. Cambridge: Harvard University Press, 1971, p. 235. Footnote 20. For a general discussion, see Lon Fuller, *The Morality of Law* (New Haven, Yale University Press, 1964), ch II. The concept of principal decisions in constitutional law is considered by Herbert Wechsler, *Principles, Politics, and Fundamental Law* (Cambridge, Harvard University Press, 1961). See Otto Kirchenheimer, *Political Justice* (Princeton, Princeton University Press, 1961), and J. N. Shklar, *Legalism* (Cambridge, Harvard University Press, 1964), pt. II, for the use and abuse of Judicial forms in politics. J. R. Lucas, *The Principles of Politics* (Oxford, The Clarendon Press, 1966), pp. 106-143, contains a philosophical account.

[276] Ibid, pp. 251-257.

Kant argues that people "express their nature as free and equal rational beings subject to the general conditions of human life."[277] That is to say, "the lives of the saint and the scoundrel are equally the outcome of free choice and equally the subject of causal laws."[278] Rawls concludes by saying, "Thus justice as fairness is a theory of human justice and among its premises are the elementary facts about persons and their place in nature."[279] Today, justice in America is based more on who has the financial ability to hire the best lawyers in a lawsuit, than Rawls' notion of the equality standard of fairness.[280]

America's *Legal System* is in need of a major overhaul.

The *Judiciary Act of 1789* "incorporated the principle of federal supremacy into the national judicial system."[281] That "Act" provided for a Supreme Court, thirteen federal district courts and three circuit courts. On February 2, 1790 the Supreme Court opened its first session in New York City. Written by Chief Justice John Marshall "The famous case of *Marbury v. Madison* in 1803" established the doctrine of judicial review and made the Supreme Court a center of power.[282]

The American Bar Association (ABA) was founded on August 21, 1878 in Saratoga Springs, New York.[283] "The ABA (is) the largest voluntary professional association in the world."[284] "With more than 400,000 members, the ABA provides law school accreditation, continuing legal education, information about the law, programs to assist lawyers and judges in their work, and initiatives to improve the legal system for the public."[285]

---

[277] Ibid, pp. 252-253.

[278] Ibid, p. 254.

[279] Ibid, p. 257.

[280] Eaglesham, Jean. Challenges in Chasing Fraud. *The Wall Street Journal*. Thursday, June 23, 2011, P. C1.

[281] Kelly, Alfred H., Harbison, Winfred A. and Belz, Herman. *The American Constitution Its Origins and Development*. New York: W. W. Norton & Company, 1991, p. 157.

[282] Ibid, p. 170. John Marshall (1755-1835) served as Chief Justice of the United States from 1801 until his death in 1835.

[283] www.abanet.org.

[284] Ibid.

[285] Ibid.

"People who manipulate the law wield the real power in society."[286]

Life experiences often trump objectivity and influence how judges (both men and women) come to arrive at decisions in legal matters. In an interview with Emily Bazelon, the Truman Capote fellow at Yale Law School, Justice Ruth Bader Ginsburg said, "...women bring a different life experience to the table. All of our differences make the conference better. That I'm a woman, that's part of it, that I'm Jewish, that's part of it, that I grew up in Brooklyn, N.Y., and I went to summer camp in the Adirondacks, all these things are part of me."[287] Justice Ginsburg's candor is refreshing. Her disclosure however, raises a serious question about the nation's judicial system in general, and *activist* federal judges in particular. The question is this:

Since all judges are the sum of their experiences and training, just like Justice Ginsburg, are they able to be dispassionate about the Constitution, law and intent of the Founders when making rulings, or do they all too often ignore the law, and decide cases based on their personal socio-political ideology? It seems that large numbers of judges view the United States Constitution as an impediment to their vision for America. As a result of their activist actions, these judges polarize the nation and bring to a near standstill needed debate on pressing problems facing the nation today.

The appointment process to the judiciary must be changed. The Senate Judiciary Committee and the ABA have failed.

The need for change extends from judicial appointments to tort reform. To ensure best standards criteria and objectivity; the selection and appointment of judges to the Supreme Court must be made from a pool of judges who have been successfully evaluated by a bi-partisan selection committee and found qualified to serve on the Supreme Court. Supreme Court appointments should have a term-limit of 15 years.

Medical malpractice lawsuits typify what's wrong with America's legal system.

Tucker Carlson is a regular columnist for *Reader's Digest*. In an article published in October 2002 entitled, <u>Sued Sick</u>, he said, "... Dr. Cheryl

---

[286] Chernow, p. 25.
[287] Bazelon, Emily. <u>The Place of Women on the Court</u>. New York: *The New York Times Magazine*, July 12, 2009, p. 24.

Edwards ... a successful ob-gyn in Las Vegas ... shuttered her practice and moved out of state."[288] Her medical malpractice insurance premium had increased five times. It was now $200,000 a year.

Carlson went on to say "The crisis is even more severe in West Virginia."[289] He pointed out that "... there is not a single neurosurgeon left in the city of Wheeling, (and) over the past two years, one out of every 20 West Virginia physicians has retired or left the state."[290] Carlson concludes his article by saying, "The average jury award in a medical malpractice case is now $3.5 million, three times what it was less than a decade ago."[291] Medical malpractice not only affected West Virginia, it has extended to other states such as nearby Maryland.

In November 2004 Liz Babiarz, a news writer for the *Frederick News-Post,* (Frederick, Maryland) noted in her column entitled, Surgeons plan to close shop, that "Five of eight general surgeons in the county say they will suspend their practice."[292] The Medical Liability Society of Maryland, the largest insurer of doctors in the state announced it would be raising its medical malpractice insurance premiums by 33 percent. This was on top of a 28 percent increase the year before. Babiarz said that "Calls to the state's top lawmakers ... were not returned."[293]

In the March/April/May 2008 issue of *Best for Women* magazine, writer Marielena Zuniga says, "As more ob-gyns leave their practices, women struggle to find maternity care."[294] She says, "Dr. Lisa Hollier, associate professor at the University of Texas, Houston, Lyndon B. Johnson Hospital Program said, 'The medical liability crisis is key'."[295] Zuniga went on to say:

> "Dr. Mary Jane Minkin, clinical professor of ob-gyn at
> Yale University School of Medicine, gave up the obstetrics
> part of her work, and now provides only gynecological

---

[288] Carlson, Tucker. Sued Sick. *Reader's Digest.* October 2002, p. 35.

[289] Ibid.

[290] Ibid.

[291] Ibid, p. 36.

[292] Babiarz, Liz. Surgeons plan to close shop. Frederick: *Frederick News-Post.* November 2004, p. A-1.

[293] Ibid, p. A-11.

[294] Zuniga, Marielena. Is There a Doctor in the House? *Best for Women.* March/April/May 2008, p. 13.

[295] Ibid, pp. 14 – 15.

services as a part of a group practice in New Haven, Connecticut. During a five-year period, she saw annual Liability insurance rates jump from \$32,000 to \$90,000 per doctor."[296]

Most law firms handle medical malpractice lawsuits on a contingency basis. That means they share in the amount of the settlement or award based on the verdict. Contingency fees typically range from 25% to 50% of that amount. Meanwhile, on their web site, the law firm of Morgan & Morgan reports that as of October 31, 2010, the organization has racked up over \$80 million in medical malpractice verdicts.[297] And that is just one of the many hundreds of thousands of lawyers who are members of the ABA who actively participate in the filing of medical malpractice lawsuits.

Litigation Reform is needed right now.

The United States is mired in a morass of legal entanglements. The power and influence the legal community and judiciary have over the nation is staggering. Mega-international law firms set the agenda and promulgate federal regulation which govern much of America and impact the lives of its citizenry. These law firms are brokering a dangerous socioeconomic and political ideology.

Because of pre-designed and required legal arrangements, a *Duoistic* United States becomes incapable of movement or action.[298] It is paralyzed when it comes to arriving at meaningful solutions to a number of important issues facing the nation today. If America's legal community is left unchecked, the United States will be rendered powerless. It will be impossible for the country to function unless it is governed by a Totalitarian leader. Understandably, to many readers this sounds farfetched.

In her book *On Revolution* Hannah Arendt says, "we shall have to keep in mind that the distance between tyranny and constitutional, limited

---

[296] Ibid.

[297] www.forthepeople.com. 10/31/2010.

[298] *Duoism* – is an emerging socioeconomic and political "ism" in America. It gained socio-political momentum in the early 1960s with the emergence of the New Left Movement. It gained economic momentum in the early 1980s during the Reagan Administration.

government is as great as, perhaps greater than, the distance between limited government and freedom."[299]

For those who remain skeptical and hold that such a happening can't occur in the United States, there is an assemblage of evidence presented in this text which argues to the contrary. It not only can happen in the United States – tyranny is subtly unfolding right now on the American landscape, and has been for quite sometime. Peace, prosperity and liberty are at stake. Americans must take swift corrective action to stem the tide. A critical and necessary step is legal reform in America.

Amendment VI. to *The* CONSTITUTION *of the* United States reads in part "... the accused shall enjoy the right to a speedy and public trial ...." Today, according to a study prepared for the Pacific Research Institute, the average lawsuit takes "...15 months to resolve; cases with punitive damage demands takes an average of 21 months to resolve."[300] Many lawsuits take years to resolve.

As a first step, the litigation process needs to be streamlined. Litigation forums need to be identified based on dollar amount of claims. The chief reason being, smaller claims are more likely to settle their differences early on, while larger claims tend to be drawn out. This provides for the courts to ably and efficiently manage their dockets. With larger claims, parties are more willing to litigate the matter. Second, dollar amounts of a lawsuit should become the criteria for determining which forum the matter will be tried. For example, lawsuits with claims up to $25,000 should be tried in a *Mediation* forum. Claims ranging from $25,001 to $100,000 would be tried in *Arbitration* forums. Only claims involving dollar amounts exceeding $100,000 would be heard in a *Court of Law.* These reforms would lighten judges' dockets in order for them to hear more complicated cases; and to permit parties to lawsuits involving lesser amounts of money to benefit from a speedy conclusion by using arbitration and mediation forums to resolve their differences.

The House Judiciary Committee should form a third-party Tort Reform Working Group. This group would have the responsibility to develop a comprehensive set of reforms involving tort actions. The group would have one year to complete its assignment. Thereafter, the House

---

[299] Arendt, Hannah. *On Revolution.* New York: The Viking Press, 1963, p. 218. Hannah Arendt (1906-1975) was a leading 20th century political theorist.

[300] Hayward, Ph.D, Steven F. The Role of Punitive Damages in Civil Litigation: New Evidence from Lawsuit Filings. *Pacific Research Institute.* 11/3/2010.

Judiciary Committee would open hearings on the issue. This window should be three months. At the conclusion, sound tort reform should be in place for later passage into law.

A mechanism has to be put in place to dissuade the filing of "frivolous and vexatious" lawsuits. As a start, financial penalties should be imposed on those who are repeat offenders. A "loser pays" or "lawyer pays" (repeat offenders) is a viable deterrent in the filing of malicious complaints. The litigation process is costly and both parties run the risk of an adverse decision. The allocation of costs and attorney's fees to the adverse party will encourage litigants to settle their differences. Those who are holdouts to a reasonable settlement offer would receive only partial indemnity costs and fees.

Political will is required in order for these needed reforms to happen. Leadership must first come from the Oval Office followed by genuine support from the ABA. College and university law schools must be an integral part of the paradigm. If the United States is to move forward effectively in the 21st century, legal reform is mandatory – it is not an option. The third villain is America's *two party system*.

The *Two Party System* in the United States is corrupt. It is ineffective as a political institution.

On June 17, 1972 five men broke into the Democratic National Committee's office located at the Watergate Complex in Washington, D.C. All five men were tied to an organization called the Committee to Re-elect the President. The committee was linked to high government officials in the Nixon Administration. This event, called *Watergate*, led to a high profile political scandal, the threat of presidential impeachment and finally the resignation of President Richard M. Nixon.

The Reagan Administration was marked by scandal. The most notorious of the many scandals which plagued the Reagan presidency was an event known as the *Iran Contra Affair*. In November 1986, President Reagan acknowledged that the United States had sold military weapons to the government of Iran in an attempt to gain the release of 52 Americans being held hostage. Some of the money from the arms sale was funneled to a revolutionary group operating in Nicaragua. The Reagan presidency never regained its prominence after this scandal became disclosed to the American people.

Bill Clinton, the 42nd President of the United States, was impeached for perjury on an obstruction of justice charge concerning his involvement with a White House aide. He was later acquitted by the U.S. Senate. This was just one more scandal, in a chain of scandals.

The early years of the 21st century were also epidemic of scandal. For example, the Administration of George W. Bush had its difficulties. It involved a CIA leak scandal, also known as the *Plame Affair*. This disgraceful event brought down Lewis "Scooter" Libby, Chief of Staff to the Vice President of the United States. Libby was indicted based on a leak of identity of CIA agent, Valerie Plame Wilson. He was convicted on obstruction of justice and perjury charges as well as making false statements. Libby would become the highest ranking White House official to be convicted of a crime, next to John Poindexter who was convicted in the Iran-Contra Affair during the Reagan Administration.

The Obama Administration would come to gain notoriety from a number of obscure sets of circumstances.[301] Anita Dunn, President Obama's White House Communications Director, "admitted that one of (her) favorite political Philosophers ... that she 'turns to most', is Mao Tse-Tung, the demonic communist dictator responsible for the starvation, torture, and murder of 70 million Chinese." Mr. Obama named Van Jones as "Green Jobs Czar." Jones, "a self-described 'communist' and who was arrested during (the) Rodney King riot" resigned under pressure.[302] At no time in the history of the United States has a President knowingly appointed a Communist to a high position in the federal government.

The RINOs

RINO is an acronym for Republican in Name Only. It refers to Republicans who typically vote with Progressive or left wing Democratic members of Congress. Senator John McCain of Arizona typifies the term, RINO. Lindsay Graham, Senator from South Carolina, is a close second.

To illustrate, eight Republicans (RINOs) voted with the Progressives in Congress for President Obama's "Cap and Trade" bill. Thirty-four Republicans voted for the "TARP" fund bailout of Wall Street bankers and supported Mr. Obama's immigration policy.

---

[301] www.orthodoxytoday.org. 1/21/2010.
[302] www.examiner.com. 1/21/2010.

Congress is out of touch with mainstream America.

The Center for Responsive Politics reports that in 2008, of the 535 members of Congress in the United States, 237, or forty-four percent (44%), were millionaires. Of the top 25 richest legislators – 14 were Democrats and 11 were Republicans. This suggests that when it comes to wealth, there is no distinction between the two political parties. Of the five richest members of Congress, one is a Republican followed by four Democrats. According to the Congressional Research Service, ninety-five percent (95%) of the members of the U.S. Congress are college graduates. This compares with twenty-seven percent (27%) of the adult population who hold a college degree. The United States Congress can be described as elite, privileged, well-educated and rich. For the most part, they are completely removed from mainstream America.

The American political system has increasingly become a one party institution comprised of likeminded and moneyed members. Their political ideological differences have become blurred. This structure leads to a very dangerous groupthink among politicians making the organization susceptible to tyrannical rule.

A striking example of this is Congresses' bailout of Wall Street. By now, many Wall Street bankers should have been prosecuted for wrongdoing, brought to justice for causing the worst financial crisis since the Great Depression and be serving time in jail. Instead, they are still in high office doing what got them into trouble in the first place – attempting to make money by entering into risky bets trading swaps and derivative products. If they fail, they arrange to have the taxpayers fund their losing trades. That is a "win, win" situation at the expense of the electorate. In other words, "the financiers have purchased the silence and acquiescence of both parties."[303]

Corruption: a hallmark of America's two-party system.

Michelle Malkin is a syndicated columnist, political commentator and author. In her book, *Culture of Corruption,* she characterizes President "Obama's team-the 'best of Washington insiders,' as David Brooks called

---

[303] Klein, Joe. America from the Road. *Time.* October, 18, 2010, p. 42.

it-is a dysfunctional and dangerous conglomerate of business-as-usual cronies."[304]

Jack Abramoff was a lobbyist during the Bush Administration. Malkin describes Abramoff as "a slimeball serving five to ten at a graybar hotel in Maryland."[305]

Two examples of corruption in America today are the Association of Community Organizations for Reform Now (ACORN) and Service Employees International Union (SEIU). Both organizations have strong ties to Washington.

ACORN was founded in 1970. It was a non-profit organization headquartered in New Orleans, Louisiana. Its mission was to provide: 1) better housing for the disadvantaged, 2) enhanced wages for the poor, 3) educational reform, 4) voter registration capability and 5) social justice matters. Forty percent of ACORN's revenue came from the American taxpayer.[306]

ACORN had "a long history of engaging in voter fraud, corporate shakedowns, partisan bullying, and pro-illegal immigrant lobbying."[307] In 2009, in light of various scandals and with strong bi-partisan support, the United States House and Senate passed legislation that prohibited the federal government from funding ACORN. Malkin says, "'ACORN is a criminal enterprise'."[308]

SEIU provides representation of workers in the healthcare, public and property services industries. The union is headquartered in Washington, DC. It has 2.2 million members. "SEIU represents the very essence of top-down corruption and business-as-usual funded by compulsory dues of its workers."[309] In 2008-2009, three of SEIU's chief "operatives were forced to step down over financial scandals."[310]

Movements must replace the two-party system in America.

George Washington warned the body politic of the danger associated with political parties emerging in America.[311] John Adams and Thomas

---

[304] Malkin, Michelle. *Culture of Corruption*. Washington, DC: Regnery Publishing. Inc., 2009, p. 5.
[305] Ibid, p. 12.
[306] Ibid, p. 231.
[307] Ibid.
[308] Ibid, p. 250.
[309] Ibid, p. 201.
[310] Ibid.
[311] Appendix B.

Jefferson echoed like sentiments.[312] In order to provide all Americans effective and transparent governance, the nation's citizenry must embark on a mission to dismantle the two-party political system in America.

Americans must be bold, shed their party affiliations with the Democratic and Republican parties, and become INDEPENDENTS.

The current political institution of the two-party system must be replaced with a number of *movements*. The *Tea Party* movement is the beginning of the dismantling of that two-party, political institution. This organization embraces the tenets of the *Founding Fathers* and the notion that the United States is a Republic anchored in the CONSTITUTION and not in political parties.

A new *Labor* movement must emerge in the United States. This movement would replace corrupt unions, champion financial and social causes for workers in business, industry and agriculture. Workers would have representation on the Board of Directors of public corporations where they work, much like the present day model in Europe. The new *Labor* movement's chief mission would be to keep jobs in America.

Similar to the *Christian Democratic Union* in Germany, the new *Christian Democratic* movement in the United States would hold central to its platform the principles of Christian democracy. It would galvanize those citizens who hold to the notion that central to the idea of America is the separation of church and state. With that said, the movement's goal would be to keep alive the historical importance the Judea-Christian influence had in the early formation of the United States.

Finally, a renewed *Business* movement would be seen as an important step in protecting the institution of private enterprise in America. The central role this movement would have is ensuring the continued prosperity of the nation's citizenry by creating new industries and jobs for Americans.

Collectively, these movements will come to replace a dysfunctional two-party political institution in America and reconstitute the core elements of the market system operating in a Republic. The current socioeconomic and political model is outdated and corrupt. It needs to be re-tooled and brought current immediately.

---

[312] McCullough, p. 422. Morison, pp. 131-135.

Duoism - an emerging Totalitarian Oligarchy in America

Relationships between business and government, both in Europe and the United States, are not new. "The joint-stock company was a type of corporation ... (which) had been used in England since the fourteenth century as an instrument of the government."[313] They can be traced directly to the medieval guild merchant. The joint-stock company was the preferred form of incorporation that was used in developing colonies in English North America.[314] Unlike the joint-stock company relationships in fourteenth century England, what is emerging in America today is a disturbing phenomenon, and the fourth villain called *Duoism*.

The emerging Duoistic society in America is portrayed as the federal government in partnership with large American banks and mega corporations who together, are in a quest for world domination. Under this arrangement, roles between government and industry are blurred. What emerges is an oligarchical arrangement governed by a small group of elite, controlling individuals whose goals are personal financial gain and power. The result of such alliances is an elite totalitarian oligarchy which presides over an increasingly dystopian society. If *Duoism* is left unchecked, it will be the knell of America.

Lockheed Martin is a paradigmatic illustration that is epicenter to the notion of *Duosim* in America.

The Lockheed Martin Corporation traces its roots to the Loughead Aircraft Manufacturing Company, formed in 1916 by Allan and Malcolm Loughead of Burbank, California.[315] Its early business platform was to manufacture passenger-flying and commercial aircraft. A Duoistic relationship between Lockheed Martin and the federal government began to emerge with the military buildup for World War II. The war itself would come to transform the entire aircraft industry.[316] "Output increased by an astounding 13,500 percent during the war: the U.S. aviation industry produced more than 300,000 aircraft for the military

---

[313] Kelly, p. 2.
[314] Ibid, pp. 2-3.
[315] Hartung, William D. *Prophets of War:* Lockheed Martin and the Making of the Military-Industrial Complex. New York: Nation Books, 2011, p. 31.
[316] Ibid, p. 51.

services."[317] The overarching question was what would the industry do once the war had ended?

The war ended in Western Europe on May 7, 1945. A few months later, Lockheed Martin's President, Robert Gross, provided testimony before the Senate Committee investigating National defense Programs. Gross told the members of that committee, that "the aircraft industry had answered the nation's call during wartime-providing America with the 'greatest air force in the world, and a production capacity of 50,000 planes per year'-the U.S. government had an obligation to sustain the industry in peacetime."[318] Gross outlined what he wanted from his new business partner, the federal government. He wanted the government to:

> "give the production equipment it had paid for during the war to industry on a free or low-cost basis. Gross argued that it would otherwise be sold for scrap with little benefit to the government. He also wanted to avoid having the government dump military transport planes onto the commercial market, a move that would deprive Lockheed and its cohorts of potential business. And he wanted the development of a peacetime aviation policy that would provide subsidies in areas such as support for civilian transport planes that could be converted to military use in time of war."[319]

Many on the committee were sympathetic to Gross's position. "Senator Edwin Johnson of Colorado was not."[320] He expressed his concerns this way. He said:

> "The kind of planning that Gross was propounding would lead to 'a totalitarian system' in which Lockheed 'had one customer, and that customer was Uncle Sam, with bags and bags of money.' Instead, he suggested a return to the free enterprise model that had existed before World War II. Gross countered and said, that lack of planning was what could bring 'a totalitarian system in this country or

---

[317] Ibid.
[318] Ibid, p. 52.
[319] Ibid, p. 53.
[320] Ibid, p. 58.

something worse,' presumably referring to the possible conquest of the United States if it let it's guard down by failing to sustain its edge in air power'."[321]

"This practice of equating the aircrafts industry's interests with the national interest was to serve Lockheed and its rivals well in the decades to come."[322] The foundation of *Duoism* had been laid.

Today, Lockheed Martin does everything from oversight responsibility for the printing of census forms to processing data at banks of computer terminals. The company helps sort the people's mail. Lockheed Martin's government contracts evidence the firm is involved at "one level or another in nearly everything the federal government does, from providing instruments of death and destruction to collecting taxes and recruiting spies."[323] The Duoist partnership forged in 1945 by Lockheed Martin and the United States of America is well positioned on into the 21st century.

In her book, *The Origins of TOTALITARIANISM*, Hannah Arendt argues that repeatedly, evidence supports the notion that "totalitarian governments aspire to conquer the globe and bring all countries on earth under their domination."[324] "Totalitarian domination ... aims at abolishing freedom ...."[325] Arendt holds the tenets of totalitarianism include: 1) propaganda, 2) indoctrination, 3) terror, 4) the acquisition of power through organization, and 5) the power of the federal government's leader becomes the 'supreme law' – replacing the nation's Constitution.[326]

Totalitarian *Duoism* is anchored in Marxist-Socialist ideology. The body politic is denied of justice, peace and prosperity. Liberty is lost. The method of governance is tyranny.

"Lying" is a chief tenet of Totalitarian leadership.

Honesty builds trust among people. Dishonesty is wicked behavior. "One of the important differences between a totalitarian movement and a totalitarian state is that the totalitarian dictator can and must practice the totalitarian art

---

[321] Ibid.

[322] Ibid, p. 59.

[323] Ibid, p. 247.

[324] Arendt, Hannah. *The Origins of TOTALITARIANISM*. New York: The World Publishing Company, 1958, p. 415.

[325] Ibid p. 405.

[326] Ibid, pp. 344, 359, 363-364.

of lying ...."[327] "Systematic lying to the whole world can be safely carried out only under the conditions of totalitarian rule, where the fictitious quality of everyday reality makes propaganda largely superfluous."[328]

Presidential candidates and Presidents of the United States have sharpened their skills of lying to the American people. During the 2008 presidential campaign, Senator Hillary Clinton told a story of how she managed to dodge sniper fire while on a trip to Tuzla, Bosnia, in 1996. She said, "'I remember landing under sniper fire,' she said gravely in a speech at George Washington University in March 2008."[329] "When a video of the cherry greeting ceremony surfaced in March 2008 showing no such thing, Hillary's excuses poured forth. She 'misspoke'."[330]

Barack Obama had proudly made much reference to his ties to ACORN. Later, presidential candidate Obama "asserted on its 'Fight the Smears' campaign website that he 'never organized with ACORN'."[331] "According to ACORN, however, Obama trained its Chicago members in leadership seminars; in turn, ACORN volunteers worked on his campaign."[332] The truth is once again obfuscated

Spreading falsehoods is a two way street. During his Nevada victory speech (February 5, 2012) Mitt Romney said "Obama told the people the stimulus would hold unemployment below 8%." This is not an accurate representation of what was said. While Obama's advisors were wrong in their projections, President Obama never held to the notion that 8% unemployment was a fixed number.

Lying is a trait that must come easy and naturally for totalitarian leaders. Their goal is to move the *Duoistic* agenda at all costs. The Republic, the citizenry and liberty – those attributes are for another "time" and "place" in American history. Those thoughts are anchored in the past. *Duoism* looks to the now and the future.

Duoism in Action.

Duoism transcends political party lines. It believes so passionately in the wisdom of its self-centered vision, that the ends justify the means.

---

[327] Ibid, p. 413.
[328] Ibid.
[329] Malkin, pp. 253-254.
[330] Ibid, p. 254.
[331] Ibid, p. 231.
[332] Ibid.

George W. Bush championed a "New World Order." Barack Obama's campaign mantra was – "Change, yes we can." In the fall of 2007, Obama made "one of his most important campaign speeches."[333] At the climax of his speech, Obama asked the crowd, "'Fired up?' The frenzied crowd responded 'Fired up!' When asked, 'Ready to go?' they responded, 'Ready to go!'"[334]

Obama then "exhorted them:

'Let's go change the world!'"[335]

Obama called for "change." His directive was to "change the world." This is *Totalitarian* in nature and Obama's rhetoric comes directly from the Marxist playbook.[336]

Grounded in Marxist-Socialist ideology, there is persuasive evidence that the United States is on a *Duoistic* path toward Totalitarian Rule by an Elite Oligarchy.

For those readers who continue to find the argument that the United States is vulnerable to totalitarian governance unthinkable – the following incident which occurred during the Bush Administration provides enlightenment. It offers persuasive evidence to all Americans, that the notion of totalitarianism and tyrannical governance is not something to be taken lightly. It is a very real threat to this nation and to the well-being of its citizenry.

To illustrate:

> "George W. Bush signed the Defense Authorization Act in a private Oval office ceremony. Tucked into its fourteen hundred pages is a rider that went almost completely unnoticed at the time. It gave the president the power to declare martial law and 'employ the armed forces, including the National Guard,' overriding the wishes of

---

[333] Ibid, p. 195.
[334] Ibid, p. 196.
[335] Ibid. Arendt, p. 415.
[336] "Philosophers have only interpreted the world; the point is to change it." By: Karl Marx: "… the last of his eleventh theses on the German materialist philosopher Ludwig Feuerbach." Puchner, Martin. (ed.). *The Communist Manifesto and Other Writings*. New York: Barns & Noble Classics, 2005, pp. xxviii- xxix.

state governors, in the event of a 'public emergency' in order to 'restore public order' and 'suppress' the disorder. That emergency could be a hurricane, a mass protest or a 'public health emergency,' in which case the army could be used to impose quarantines and to safeguard vaccine supplies. Before this act, the president had these martial law powers only in the face of an insurrection."[337]

Turning to the idea of a *Duoistic* oligarchy involving corporate America and the federal government, prior to Dick Cheney becoming Vice president of the United States, Halliburton's revenues from U.S. government contracts was 5%. In 2003, the percent of Halliburton's revenues from government work had increased to 26%.[338] Recall, Dick Cheney was the former CEO of Halliburton.

Cisco Systems gets 22% of its income from the public sector.[339] The federal government owns 61% of General Motors, 36% of Citigroup and $69.8 billion in preferred shares of AIG. The federal government also owns 650 million acres of land – almost 30% of the land area of the entire United States.[340]

In another instant, Clean Energy Fuels is a company that has had a partner relationship with the United States government for sometime. The organization provides fuels for natural gas-powered trucks. As an incentive, the federal government provided Clean Energy with an alternative-fuel tax credit. Without such an arrangement, the company would be unprofitable despite unsustainably high gross margins on its fuel sales. Recently, "Senate Majority Leader Harry Reid canceled a scheduled vote on his proposal for further rebates on natural-gas-powered trucks."[341] Without the alternative-fuel tax credit, the future of Clean Energy Fuels is anyone's guess.

The testimonies of corporate arrangements with the federal government are endless. These are but a few examples to make the point.

---

[337] Klein, Naomi. *The Shock Doctrine*, pp. 308-309.

[338] www.informingvoters.org.

[339] Galante, Joseph and Thomson, Amy. Government cutbacks rouse bleak forecast from Cisco Systems. *Washington Post.* Thursday, November 11, 2010.

[340] www.nationalatlas.gov.

[341] Alpert, Bill. Picken's Clean Energy Stock Runs Out of Gas. *Barron's.* November 22, 2010, p. 19.

America is embarking on a *Duoistic* system of government which can only end in the nation's governance changing radically for the worse.

The heart of all industrial economies is *the making of things*.[342]

The notion of "the making of things" remained true for the longest time. However, in the early 1980s American corporations came to realize they could have their products manufactured abroad at a substantial cost-savings; bring the final product back to the United States, brand it, and sell that finished item at a substantial mark-up to the citizenry.

Naomi Klein, an activist best known for her political analyses, is a critic of corporate globalization. In her book, *No Logo*, she discloses a number of American corporations whose business plans today avoid any discussion of their own workforce or manufacturing techniques. Klein points out that corporate business plans today focus on design, brand management and marketing of the finished product. Here's how it works.

American companies partnership with host country governments. These countries include such places as "China, Mexico, Vietnam, the Philippines and elsewhere."[343] They establish what are called Free-Trade Zones (FTZ). The majority of workers which comprise the cheap, non-union workforce assemblies in the FTZ are women.[344] Rent for factories is cheap in the FTZ and companies regularly cheat on their workers.[345] For example, companies will promise a certain income to workers, and then find ways to garnish their wages. In one instance, a company charged employees to go to the bathroom. The endgame is clear. Manufacture a product overseas as cheaply as possible, return it to America; brand it and market the product aggressively to the American consumer.

In another of her books entitled, *The Shock Doctrine,* Klein identifies an activity which describes the core process which is logocentric to the notion of *Duoism*. Here, she replaces the "revolving door" with an "archway." Based on this concept, rather than coming and going through a revolving door, people move continuously back and forth – between industry and the federal government in a linear fashion. These are the people who form the oligarchial elite. They make the rules; go back to industry and implement

---

[342] Klein, Naomi. *No Logo*. New York: Picador, 2002, p. 4.
[343] Ibid, p. 202.
[344] Ibid, pp. 205 and 207.
[345] Ibid, p. 211.

those rules and profit by the exercise. If the rules need to be changed to keep the "gig" going, they pass through the archway, return to Washington and the process starts all over again. Klein explains it this way:

"Vice president Dick Cheney was ... reluctant to fully sever his ties to Halliburton-an arrangement that ...has been the subject of a great deal of media attention. Before stepping down as CEO to be George Bush's running mate, Cheney negotiated a retirement package that left him loaded with Halliburton stocks and options. After some uncomfortable press questions, he agreed to sell some of his Halliburton shares, making an impressive $18.5 million profit in the process. But he didn't cash out entirely. According to *The Wall Street Journal,* Cheney hung on to 189,000 Halliburton shares and 500,000 unvested options even as he entered the vice presidency.

The fact that Cheney still maintains such a quantity of Halliburton shares means that throughout his term as vice president, he has collected millions every year in dividends from his stocks and has also been paid an annual deferred income by Halliburton of $211,000-roughly equivalent to his government salary. When he (left) office in 2009 he was able to cash in his Halliburton holdings, (and had) the opportunity to profit extravagantly from the stunning improvement in Halliburton's fortunes. The company's stock price rose from $10 before the war in Iraq to $41 three years later-a 300 percent jump, thanks to a combination of soaring energy prices and Iraq contracts, both of which flow directly from Cheney's steering the country into war with Iraq."[346]

Being in an elite position of power and special favor can lead to obtaining privileged communication thereby achieving extraordinary personal financial gain.

On February 6, 2009, Bank of America corporate insider Thomas M. Ryan purchased 25,000 shares of Bank of America stock at $5.60. That same

---

[346] Klein, *The Shock Doctrine,* p. 313.

day, insiders Brian T. Moynihan and Walter Massey purchased 10,000 shares at $4.80 and 2,000 shares at $6.21 respectively. On February 17, 2009, insider Jacquelyn Ward purchased 9,900 shares at $5.05 and again on February 20, 2009, she bought 13,100 shares at $3.78. On November 26, 2010, Bank of America stock closed at $11.12 a share.[347]

On March 3, 2009, four Citigroup insiders made purchases of the bank's stock. Lewis B. Kaden purchased 100,000 shares at $1.26. Manuel Medina purchased 1.5 million shares at $1.24. John C. Gerspach purchased 65,000 shares at $1.20 and Roberto Hernandez bought 6 million shares at $1.25. On November 26, 2010, Citigroup stock closed at $4.11 a share.[348]

On March 2, 2009, four General Electric insiders bought shares in General Electric stock. Jeffrey Immelt purchased 50,000 shares at $8.89. Claudio Gonzalez bought 20,000 shares at $7.00 and Samuel A. Nunn, Jr., purchased 30,000 shares at $7.00. Michael Neal bought 50,000 shares at $7.90 a share. On November 26, 2010, the shares of General Electric stock closed at $15.80 a share.[349]

There certainly is nothing illegal about insiders purchasing shares of stock in the company in which they are affiliated - providing they comply with the required SEC regulations pertaining to such transactions. That being said, what is ironic in these illustrations – is that all of these insiders were from three different companies. How they would have timed their purchases on these particular dates, and all having made their purchases at or near historic lows reflecting extraordinary personal financial gains based on recent closing prices – the explanation to these observations would be most interesting to find out.

In her book *On Revolution* Arendt highlights "the enormous role the social question has come into play in all revolutions...."[350] She writes "that Aristotle ... discovered the importance of what we call today economic motivation – the overthrow of government by the rich and the establishment of an oligarchy, or the overthrow of government by the poor and the establishment of a democracy?"[351]

---

[347] Appendix K.
[348] Appendix L.
[349] Appendix M.
[350] Arendt, Hannah. *On Revolution,* p. 21.
[351] Ibid, p. 22.

Americans must come together and dismantle the emerging Totalitarian Duoistic Oligarchy in the United States.

America has got to get back to "making things." The nation's job market must be restored to greatness. This can be done by: 1) providing tax incentives to corporations who create and keep jobs in the United States and 2) imposing tax penalties on those organizations who export jobs abroad. Executive compensation should be tied to job creation at home.

Small business is the engine that drives the nation's economy. Incentives such as low interest loans and tax benefits should be made available to organizations such as McDonald's and Diary Queen who spin off company owned outlets to private business ownership. This concept could even be extended to such enterprises as Home Depot and Wal-Mart. What emerges from this paradigm is a nation of family owned businesses across the nation.

In order to accommodate such an arrangement, it is mandatory that America's banking system be restored to soundness. As a first step, the Duocratic oligarchy which operates the nation's largest banks needs to be dismantled. The country's ten largest financial institutions registered as banks should be broken up now. Second, the emerging model will be in the image of the intended consequences of the Glass-Steagall Act.

America's legal system is in disarray. It is in need of immediate reform. Steps should be taken to: 1) establish a series of hearing venues to ensure parties to a lawsuit have access to a speedy litigation process, 2) engage in tort reform and 3) develop a penalty matrix for those persons who file frivolous lawsuits.

The nation's political party system is in shambles. It is beyond repair. Americans must formally reject the corrupt two-party political structure in the United States. This can only be done if the body politic, en masse, switches their political party affiliation from either Democrat or Republican – as the case may be, to *Independent*. This is a major step in America "Returning to First Principles."

Finally, all traces of political correctness must be removed from education curricula. This tyrannical method of speech and writing prohibits needed discussion and action about pressing issues facing the nation today. This Marxist control technique must be abolished from the American landscape.

CHAPTER EIGHT

A SOCIETY IN REBELLION

*Those who make peaceful revolution impossible will
make violent revolution inevitable.*
                                                    -John F. Kennedy (1917-1963)

The Constitution is a legal document. It provides for the Liberty
and protection of all peoples in a Republic. "A people are a people
(and) the true foundation of society."[352] "The law of majority rule is itself
an established convention."[353] "Freedom is asserted to consist in the
individuals of a State all agreeing in its arrangements," but "the minority
must yield to the majority; the majority therefore bears the sway."[354]

The United States Census Bureau reported that as of January 3,
2012, the population of the United States was 313 million people. Of
that distribution:

- 65.2% were White.
- 16.3% were Hispanic or Latino ethnicity.
- 12.6% were Black or African American.
- 4.8% were Asian.
- 1.1% were American Indian, Pacific Islander or Other.

Voluntary selected self-reported Religious affiliation to the United
States Census Bureau reveals the following as of the reporting years and
sample size:

---

[352] Rousseau, p. 147.
[353] Ibid.
[354] Hegel, p. 43.

The twenty year reporting period: 1990 – 2010.

- 76.0% Total Christian.
- 25.1% Catholic.
- 50.9% Non-Catholic Christian.
- 1.2% Jewish.
- 0.6% Muslim.
- 1.6% Agnostic-Atheist.
- 15.4% None.
- 5.2% No Reply.

The United States is a major world power. It is located on the continent of North America. As of 2010, the population of the country was 309 million people. The demographics of the United States have not changed materially since 2006. Huntington describes the nation's citizenry as a diversified culture which is Caucasian-Christian dominant.[355] Regarding sociopolitical matters, forty percent (40%) of Americans describe themselves as *Conservative*, thirty-five percent (35%) as *Moderate* and twenty percent (20%) as *Liberal*.[356]

There are four chief reasons why America is on the brink of rebellion. First, since the early 1960s, the Progressive movement has gained a disproportionate amount of power and influence in American politics. They occupy key positions in both states and the federal government. They maintain a disproportionate representation of judgeships in America.

Second, Conservatives have failed in developing a sustainable political platform to meet the Progressive challenge. They have become distracted and allowed themselves to be "bullied" by their opposition. Progressives use Communist tactics. They often borrow from Hitler's Nazi playbook and at other times Mussolini's Fascism, to "shout down" and degrade their political opponents to win elections.

> ***Conservatives have become the softy on
> the playground. They don't fight back.***

Third, a growing number of Americans (Progressives and Conservatives) have become frustrated with the direction taken by the antiquated

---

[355] Huntington, pp. 11 and 82.
[356] www.gallup.com. June 15, 2009.

two-party system. With the decay of numerous venerable American institutions and rampant corruption in business and government they have become disillusioned with society in general. For them the circle is closed. With an economic crisis caused by reckless Wall Street bankers trading risky derivative products and near absent any form of responsible federal government regulation, these Americans have abandoned the formal political process and have opted to become *Independent*.

Fourth, "the division of (American) society into fixed ethnicities nourishes a culture of victimization and a contagion of inflammable sensitivities."[357] Schlesinger notes that "History is littered with the wreck of states that tried to combine diverse ethnic or linguistic or religious groups within a single sovereignty."[358]

Like many Progressives and Conservatives, Independents are awakening to the fact that they too are rapidly becoming increasingly disenfranchised from the *idea* of America. The majority voice of the American people is no longer being heard and herein lays the template for massive socioeconomic and political rebellion in the United States.[359]

Philosopher George Wilhelm Friedrich Hegel argued that "in large empires, diverse and conflicting interests are sure to present themselves."[360] Hegel holds that when individuality is asserted "against the moral life of the community" the end result is corruption.[361]

Hegel identifies behaviors which are symbolic of corruption and signal that a Republic is headed for rebellion. They include: "1) election to seats in parliament by means of bribery, 2) exercise the power to sell one's vote, 3) selfish misuse of political power, 4) Subjectivity, or the unreflecting simplicity or immediacy of a particular matter, 5) principle of decay; (a) morality and (b) abstraction and 6) a jealousy of liberty."[362]

Locke argues that when "people generally (the majority) are ill-treated, that this condition lays a foundation for Rebellion."[363]

---

[357] Schlesinger, p. 118.

[358] Ibid, p. 135.

[359] Collier and Dollar, p.129.

[360] Hegel, p. 255. George Wilhelm Friedrich Hegel (1770-1831) "was the last of the main representatives of a philosophical movement known as German Idealism." (See Craig, p. 334).

[361] Ibid, p. 271

[362] Ibid, pp. 265, 267 and 271.

[363] Locke, pp. 101 and 103.

The majority of Americans are being mistreated.

Americans are not heard and are being robbed of their Liberty. They are held against their will to a Marxist unit of conformity. Americans are kept in line with their speech patterns being guided by politically correct theory. Their behavior is restricted by socialist type laws and politically favored court decisions. The pattern of such activity is revealing.

Marx and Engels were "both shrewd and bold." They developed a "new form of writing which was used by political activist(s) and theorist(s)."[364] The genre is *political correctness*. The word *change* is used to signal *social revolution*.[365] These are literary tools and code words that Progressives use to manipulate public sentiment.

"The theory of Communism is summed up in a single sentence: Abolition of private property."[366] This is the first tenet of Marxist political theory. Legislation such as the Trading with the Enemy Act of 1917 and the International Emergency Powers Act of 1977, gives power to the United States Government to confiscate property from American citizens. Thus, a number of American political leaders have flirted with these confiscatory ideas for many decades.

"Communism abolishes eternal truths. Its second tenet requires 'the abolition of all religion and all morality' instead of constituting them on a new basis; it therefore acts in contradiction to all past historical experience."[367] "The Communist revolution is the most radical rupture with traditional property relations and traditional ideas."[368]

Juxtapose the second Communist tenet requiring the abolition of religion with recent happenings in the United States and the results are staggering. The Freedom From Religion Foundation, an organization founded in 1978 of 13,000 members, boasts legal successes for achieving the following actions: "1) university graduation invocations ended at top ten university, 2) prayers stopped at public institutions, 3) public sponsorship of Nativity Pageant halted, 4) crosses downed from public land, 5) abuse by preacher exposed, 6) city sponsorship of Knights of Columbus signs ended, 7) proselytizing crossing guard fired, 8) post

---

[364] Marx, pp. xxii-xxiii.
[365] Ibid, p. xxviii.
[366] Ibid, p. 21. Yao, p. 15.
[367] Marx, p. 26.
[368] Ibid, p. 27.

office/Catholic entanglement ended, 9) de facto sports Chaplaincy stopped, 10) school Boy Scout subsidy stopped, 11) Bible proclamation rescinded, 12) illegal public help halted for 'Our Lady of the Rockies,' 13) creationism removed from city zoo, 14) discount for Catholics ended, 15) Red Rocks Easter service subsidy ended, 16) Nativity scene moved off government land, 17) Ten Commandments monuments moved from public property, 18) Ethics probe called for preaching Governor, and 19) religion removed from playground."[369]

The third tenet of the *Communist Manifesto* requires "a heavy progressive or graduated income tax."[370] The United States has a "progressive income tax.' It was first established in 1913."[371] Burton Folsom is a professor of American history at Hillsdale College. In his article, *What's Wrong with the Progressive Income Tax?* Folsom argues "The principle behind the progressive income tax-which asserts the more you earn, the larger the percentage of tax you must pay-is not what the nation's Founders wanted."[372]

The fourth tenet of the *Communist Manifesto* holds to the notion of centralization of the means of communication and transportation in the hands of the state.[373] In their text *Logic and Contemporary Rhetoric* Nancy Cavender, Professor Emeritus of the College of Marin in the English department and co-author, Howard Kahane, who died in 2001, argued that "the government has ways of restricting the freedom of the press..."[374] Some of the ways in which they do this is by "issuing prepackaged reports..." Other ways include "holding secret meetings which prevent the press from attending and by restricting access to government records."[375] Cavender and Kahane hold that "Government officials also can, and do, manipulate the news by playing favorites among reporters, leaking only to those news people who play ball in return.[376] Similarly, reporters have to be careful in press conferences not to ask

---

[369] Freedom From Religion Foundation. *Other Legal Successes*. Madison: June 13, 2009.

[370] Marx, p. 27.

[371] Folsom, Burton. *What's Wrong with the Progressive Income Tax?* Midland: Mackinac Center for Public Policy, 1999.

[372] Ibid. Note: The *Founders* did not support an income tax and the taxes they did support (Duties, Imposts and Excises) were "uniform throughout the United States." See: The CONSTITUTION of the United States Article. I. Section. 8.

[373] Marx, p. 28.

[374] Cavender, p. 276.

[375] Ibid, p. 277.

[376] Ibid.

embarrassing questions or follow-up questions; those who are too brash don't get called on in (the) future.[377]

The fifth tenet of the *Communist Manifesto* calls for the "extension of factories and instruments of production owned by the State ..."[378] The "Government Takeover of GM 'Just Short of Socialism,' Economists Say" is the headline of a CNSNews.com report by Adam Brickley.[379] Brickley notes that "there seemed to be consensus among economic experts that current government intervention in the economy is setting a dangerous precedent."[380]

Gross mismanagement and the financial crisis of the 21st century caused General Motors to file for Chapter 11 bankruptcy. This government-orchestrated bailout has cost the taxpayers $50 billion. Today, the United States owns 61% of the new General Motors. This is tantamount to a command system economy. Examples of a *command system* are the former Communist Soviet Union, North Korea and China.[381] History demonstrates that *command systems* eventually fail.

The sixth tenet of the *Communist Manifesto* includes the "centralization of credit in the hands of the State, by means of a national bank with State capital and exclusive monopoly."[382] The Emergency Economic Stabilization Act of 2008 essentially paves the way for the United States government to nationalize American banks. Under these circumstances, individuals would be essentially deprived of accumulating any personal wealth whatsoever. Robbed of their liberty, they are chained to the state's banking system.

The seventh tenet of the Communist Manifesto provides for the government's ability to make "distribution of the population over the country."[383] Kristin Carlisle is development director and policy analyst for the Texas Low Income Housing Information Service. In her article entitled, <u>It's Like You're Walking But Your Feet Ain't Going Nowhere,</u> Carlisle describes the plight and misery of thousands of people who were evacuated wholesale from their homes by the federal government and

---

[377] Ibid, p. 278.

[378] Marx, p. 28.

[379] Brickley, Adam. *Government Takeover of GM 'Just Short of Socialism,' Economists Say.* Washington: CNSNews.com. June 3, 2009.

[380] Ibid.

[381] Mankiw, pp. 9-10. Yao, p. 2.

[382] Marx, p. 28.

[383] Ibid.

redistributed to Texas after Hurricane Katrina.[384] The situation was dire, but the method used to make this distribution of people geographically (a wholesale evacuation of Hurricane Katrina victims by the federal government) is a stark reminder of just how close this country is to being on the brink of authoritarian rule.

The evidence is quite clear. The United States is moving rapidly in the direction of a Duoistic socioeconomic model. American families are in shambles. For decades now, religion in America has been a slaughter-bench. Nationalism is under attack from every direction. The notion that to say the pledge of allegiance to the flag or singing the Star Spangle Banner in public can be found 'objectionable' is absolutely preposterous. The income tax policy in America is Progressive in nature. The bank bailout program and the federal government's involvement with General Motors are actions which are reminiscent of two key tenets of the *Communist Manifesto*.

Today's socioeconomic and political turbulence has caused some state officials to raise the subject of secession. This discussion has also been considered seriously by recognized academicians. For example, Huntington writes:

> "America with only the *Creed* as a basis for unity could soon evolve into a loose confederation of ethnic, racial, cultural, and political groups, with little or nothing in common apart from their location in the territory of what had been the United States of America. This could resemble the collections of diverse groups that once constituted the Austro-Hungarian, Ottoman and Russian empires."[385]

A preview as to what the Progressive agenda has planned for the United States can be seen in the award winning movie *Doctor Zhivago*.[386] The film describes the life experiences of a Russian medical doctor during the Bolshevik Revolution. It depicts the confiscation of private property, the loss of personal freedom and the cruel living conditions under a Marxist Dictator. It becomes clear, that once Communist tyranny topples

---

[384] Carlisle, Kristin. It's Like You're Walking But Your Feet Ain't Going Nowhere. Texas: National Housing Institute, Issue #147, Fall 2006.
[385] Huntington, p. 19
[386] David Lean. *Doctor Zhivago*. DVD. Hollywood: MGM, 1965.

a Republic, the chain of bondage is so strong it can only be broken by a prolonged and painful rebellion.

Hannah Arendt has this to say about rebellion and revolution.

> "If ... one keeps in mind that the end of rebellion is liberation, while the end of revolution is the foundation of freedom, the political scientist at least will know how to avoid the pitfall of the historian who tends to place his emphasis upon the first and violent stage of rebellion and liberation, on the uprising against tyranny, to the detriment of the quieter second stage of revolution and constitution, because all the dramatic aspects of his story seem to be contained in the first stage and, perhaps, also because the turmoil of liberation has so frequently defeated the revolution."[387]

She explains;

> "The basic misunderstanding lies in the failure to distinguish between liberation and freedom; there is nothing more futile than rebellion and liberation unless they are followed by the constitution of the newly won freedom."[388]

Arendt summarizes the message of this text by explaining what it means to return to First Principles. By reflecting on the 'Glorious Revolution' in England – she said the term "was not thought of as a revolution at all, but as a restoration ... (to the nation's) former righteousness and glory."[389] Return to First Principles is certainly **not** about "Change" nor is it about revolution in the literal sense. It is about restoring America to its former goodness and greatness as a major world power.

That being said, all Americans, however, must be mindful that should major resistance be implemented by the Progressive Socialists to achieve this end - then "Whenever it comes right down to a question of defending Americanism and our constitutional rights, it's justifiable to set aside ordinary procedure."[390]

---

[387] Arendt, *On Revolution,* p. 142.
[388] Ibid.
[389] Ibid, p. 43.
[390] Lewis, Sinclair. *Main Street.* New York: Barnes & Noble Classics, 2003, p. 481.

PART IV

THE UNITED STATES OF AMERICA –
A REPUBLIC IN PERPETUITY

Wherever public spirit prevails, liberty is secure.
-Noah Webster (1758-1843)

A Constitution is made for people of fundamentally differing views.
-Justice Oliver Wendell Holmes (1841-1935)

A disordered currency is one of the greatest political evils.
-Daniel Webster (1782-1852)

The United States shall guarantee to every State in this Union a Republican Form of Government.
Article. IV. Section. 4.
The CONSTITUTION of the United States of America

CHAPTER NINE

LIBERTY AND THE CONSTITUTION

The American experiment is the most tremendous and far reaching engine of social change which has ever either blessed or cursed mankind.
-Charles Francis Adams (1807-1886)

In order for America to *Return to First Principles*, it is important for it's citizenry to have a basic understanding of the mechanics and workings of the Constitution. The original work was not perfect. Over the years amendments and court interpretations were required to meet the evolving needs of the nation.

At the Philadelphia Convention in 1787 vigorous and sometimes heated debates were integral parts of the developmental process. Compromise was essential in launching the new government. Although most of the Founding Fathers were satisfied with their accomplishments in Philadelphia, some viewed the Constitution and the newly established federal government with tepidness and fear.

What were their concerns? Were they well founded? What lessons can be learned by examining the relationship between the Constitution and liberty? Can these lessons facilitate a *Return to First Principles*?

Since the Pilgrims landed at Plymouth Rock in December 1620, *Liberty* has been central to the American people's persona. Bernard Bailyn is professor of history at Harvard University. In his book *The Peopling of British North America* he says that because of the availability of entrepreneurship, economic betterment and religious toleration, "a massive, global movement of people to North America" took place.[391] People immigrated to America because they were in search for: 1) civil freedom, 2) religious freedom or 3) both.

Archibald MacLeish defined freedom as "the right to choose: the right to create for yourself the alternatives of choice."[392] "Without the possibility of choice and the exercise of choice a man is not a man but a member, an instrument, a thing."[393]

In his *Concept of Liberty*, Rawls discussed liberty in connection with "constitutional and legal restrictions."[394] In these instances, he held that "liberty is a certain structure of institutions, a certain system of public rules defining rights and duties."[395] Rawls thought "that the basic liberties must be assessed as a whole, as one system."[396] He argued that "when the liberties are left unrestricted they collide with one another."[397] In other words, "without the acceptance of reasonable procedures of inquiry and debate, freedom of speech loses its value."[398] Rawls held that "liberty is unequal as when one class of persons has a greater liberty than another or liberty is less extensive than it should be."[399] He acknowledged that the "worth of liberty is not the same for everyone."[400] Some people hold positions of power and wealth providing them the means to achieve their goals and objectives. Others are not so fortunate.

De Vattel said, "that all men inherit from nature a perfect liberty and independence, of which they cannot be deprived without their own consent."[401] He cautioned however, that "we should take care not to extend this liberty beyond its just bounds."[402] In other words, society and governments must come together and agree on certain limitations as to how far liberty should be extended within the polity.

George Washington was the first President of the United States.

---

[391] Bailyn, Bernard. *The Peopling of British North America*. New York: Vintage Books, 1986, pp. 4-5.

[392] Peter, Laurence J. *Peter's Quotations*. New York: Bantam Books, 1977, p. 199. Archibald MacLeish (1892-1982) was an American writer, poet and former Librarian of Congress.

[393] Peter, p. 199.

[394] Rawls, p. 202.

[395] Ibid.

[396] Ibid, p. 203.

[397] Ibid.

[398] Ibid.

[399] Ibid, p. 204.

[400] Ibid.

[401] Haakonssen, p. 68.

[402] Ibid, p. 157.

He held that liberty was the basis of our "independence and national character."[403]

Benjamin Franklin was one of the most revered of the Founding Fathers. He cautioned that "nothing is more likely to endanger the liberty of the press than the abuse of that liberty by employing it in personal accusation, detraction, and calumny."[404]

Thomas Jefferson, the chief author of the Declaration of Independence and third President of the United States, said "Our attachments to no nation upon earth should supplant our attachment to liberty."[405] James Madison was the fourth President of the United States. He held "that the growth and expansion of the new United States was synonymous with the spread of liberty and the rights of man."[406]

Lasting symbols of liberty are scattered throughout the American landscape. They include, among other things, the: 1) Liberty Bell, 2) Statue of Liberty, 3) American Flag, 4) American Bald Eagle and 5) Boston Freedom Trail.

The notion of *The CONSTITUTION of the* United States of America raises a number of questions. First, what is Constitutionalism? Second, what is the purpose of the American Constitution? Other questions include, who wrote the Constitution and how did it originate? How does the Constitution establish a framework for the governance of the United States? Finally, is the Constitution a lasting and unchanging document, or does it evolve on an ever changing socioeconomic and political landscape?

What is CONSTITUTIONALISM?

"Constitutionalism comprises a set of ideas, principles and rules, all of which deal with the question of how to develop a political system which excludes as far as possible the chance of arbitrary rule. While according to one of the classic sources of constitutionalism, article sixteen of the 1789 French Declaration of the

---

[403] Parry, p. 391.

[404] Skousen, Ph.D., Mark. (ed.). *The Completed Autobiography by Benjamin Franklin.* Washington, DC: Regnery Publishing, Inc., 2007, p. 377.

[405] Randall, William Sterne. *Thomas Jefferson: A Life.* New York: Harper Collins *Publishers,* 1993, p. 244.

[406] Ketcham, p. 97.

Rights of Man and of the Citizen, 'any society in which rights are not guaranteed, or in which the separation of powers is not defined, has no constitution', the scope of constitutional principles is in fact broader. In addition to these two defining principles, the following are essential: popular sovereignty; the rule of law; rules about the selection of power-holders and about their accountability to the ruled; and principles about the making, unmaking, revision, interpretation and enforcement of a constitution. Despite close affiliations, constitutionalism and democracy are not the same. Whereas democracy is an institutional device which realizes the right of the people to govern themselves, constitutionalism aims to establish institutional restraints on the power of the rulers, even if they are popularly elected and legitimized. Constitutionalism embodies the self-rationalizing and self-restraining principles of popular government."[407]

ULRICH K. PREUB[408]

What is the purpose of the American Constitution?

De Vattel posits that every political society must establish a public authority to regulate their common affairs.[409] "The fundamental regulation that determines the manner in which public authority is to be executed, is what forms the *constitution of the state.*"[410]

The public authority establishes laws which are to be observed in society. Laws affecting public welfare are called *political laws*. Laws describing "the form of government, the manner in which the public authority is to be exerted,-those, in a word, which together form the constitution of the state, are the *fundamental laws.*"[411]

---

[407] Craig, p. 147.
[408] Ulrich K. PreuB is a Professor of Public Law and Politics at Freie Universitat Berlin. He teaches Theories of the State at the Hertie School of Governance.
[409] Haakonssen, p. 91.
[410] Ibid.
[411] Ibid, p. 92.

"The constitution and laws of a state are the basis of the public tranquility, the firmest support of political authority, and a security for the liberty of the citizens."[412]

Because there were serious problems with the Articles of Confederation, Washington called for the establishment of "a 'federal constitution'."[413] He believed this document would "strengthen the national government" and "give consistency, stability, and dignity to the Union...."[414] John Adams "saw the Constitution as the best means possible 'to cement all America in affection and interest as one great nation'."[415] Not all of the *Founding Fathers* agreed on the proposed Constitution.

Jefferson objected to the Constitution on a number of issues. Among other things, he "was opposed to the notion of a powerful president" and "feared a trend away from civil liberties in America toward despotism...."[416] On the other hand, Madison looked to "the new federal constitution (as having) the sanction of supreme law...."[417] Another *Founding Father* was James Monroe. Although he "fell under the spell" of the anticonstitutionalists, "Monroe said he was 'strongly impressed with the necessity of a firm national government'."[418] On September 17, 1787, 30 of the original 55 delegates signed the Constitution. Washington was the first person to sign the document.

Who wrote the Constitution?
And
How did it originate?

The War of Independence in America was between the United States and Great Britain. Officially, it began on July 4, 1776. Essentially, the war ended on October 17, 1781 when the Commander of British forces, Lord Cornwallis, surrendered his troops at Yorktown, Virginia. There were however, some naval operations and land skirmishes which continued until November 1782. The war ended on January 20, 1783 with the signing of the *Treaty of Paris*.

Franklin was appointed Minister to France in 1776. He was seventy

---

[412] Ibid, p. 93.
[413] Parry, p. 439.
[414] Ibid, pp. 438.
[415] McCullough, p. 380.
[416] Randall, pp. 481-482.
[417] Ketcham, p. 188.
[418] Unger, Harlow Giles. *The Last Founding Father*. Philadelphia: Da Capo Press, 2009, pp. 79-80.

years old when he landed in Paris on December 3rd of that year. Franklin was instrumental in concluding a peace treaty between England and the United States. Specifically, "the preliminaries of peace between France, Spain and Great Britain were signed on January 20, 1783, and a cessation of arms agreed to by the ministers of those powers and by us in behalf of the United States."[419] The Revolutionary War and the Treaty of Paris gave birth to a new nation – the United States of America.

"The American Constitution is the final and climactic expression of the ideology of the American Revolution."[420] On May 25, 1787, the Federal Convention opened in the Old State House in Philadelphia.[421] Twelve states were represented by 55 delegates.[422] "The Virginia delegation had prepared a plan of government that served as a starting point for the convention's deliberation."[423] Madison was the chief architect of that plan which later would come to be known as the Virginia Plan.

The Virginia Plan provided:

> "a 'National Executive,' a 'National Judiciary,' and a 'National Legislature' of two branches, with members of both House and Senate apportioned according to population, empowered 'to Legislate in all cases to which the separate States are incompetent.' As to the basic question of how the states could be persuaded to abide by these Articles of Union, the Virginia plan offered three solutions: an oath of office, a negative on all state laws contravening the Constitution, and power to call forth the forces of the Union to coerce recalcitrant states."[424]

The "Virginia Plan" became "the basic framework for the document that became the Constitution of the United States."[425] Madison's labors "earned for him the title Father of the Constitution...."[426]

---

[419] Skousen, p. 283.

[420] Bailyn, *The Ideological Origins of the American Revolution*, p. 321.

[421] Morison, p. 115.

[422] Ibid, p. 114. Kelly, p. 88. (In May 1787, delegates from seven states were represented. By July, twelve states were represented.)

[423] Ibid.

[424] Morison, p. 115.

[425] Ketcham, p. 188.

[426] Ibid, p. 303.

In September, the convention appointed a committee to produce a finished product.[427] The committee included Alexander Hamilton, William Samuel Johnson, and Rufus King. It was headed by Gouverneur Morris, a Pennsylvanian.[428] "The actual task of drafting the final version was performed by Morris."[429] It is said that, Morris was the one who actually transcribed the Constitution.

By December 1788, the Congress of the Confederation had declared the new Constitution operational. Arrangements were made for the first elections in January 1789 and New York was selected as the first capital of the new government.

Some concerns.

A number of theoretical governing problems were present at the Federal Convention. These issues existed among many competing interests such as: "ethnic diversities, religious backgrounds, social distinctions and disparities of wealth."[430] There were differences over commercial interests, land speculation, slavery and credit which influenced the various proposals for structure of government. These matters required compromise of principle as well as of interests in many instances. Chief concerns among many present at the Federal Convention included, among other things, such things as: a Bill of Rights, fear of a powerful federal government, states' rights, taxation and taxing powers, executive power, the expanded role of the judiciary, defense and standing armies and coinage.[431] A pressing issue for many was the notion of a Bill of Rights.

Bill of Rights

Most state constitutions began with a 'Declaration' of some sort – a "Bill" of Rights.[432] The Virginia constitution was the paradigm. Using tenets developed by Montesquieu, Virginia's Bill of Rights addressed such issues as: freedom of the press, majority rule, freedom of speech, and the right to bear arms. Other states enlarged the list by drawing on the "Bill of

---

[427] Kelly, p. 101.

[428] Ibid, pp.101-102.

[429] Ibid, p. 101.

[430] Ketcham, Ralph. *The Anti-Federalist Papers and the Constitutional Convention Debates*. New York: Signet Classic, 2003, p. 8.

[431] Ibid, p. 27.

[432] Morison, p. 98.

Rights of 1689-freedom of assembly, of petition, right of writ of habeas corpus and equal operation of the law."[433] The first ten Amendments to the Constitution of the United States are the Bill of Rights. They were ratified effective December 15, 1791.

America's Commercial Base.

The United States would come to operate economically what is commonly referred to as the market system, or capitalism. This form of economic structure provides for the supply and demand of goods and services to be governed by open market forces. Competitive price discovery within markets would be the determining force for the distribution of products and labor. Central to this form of commercial and economic structure is a sound banking system.

The Constitution and Early America's Banking System.

Most of colonial America's economy ran on the barter system.[434] This method of exchange for goods and services was due to a "perpetual shortage of cash...before the Revolution."[435] Thereafter, and throughout the revolutionary war period, persistent problems arose in adequately funding the economy and war effort.

For example, in the winter of 1777 at Valley Forge, General George Washington noted his army's suffering. He saw "men without clothes... blankets...shoes...and he begged Congress to take action to relieve the army's horrible condition."[436] By "January 1778, a shortage of money had made necessary clumsy taxes in kind."[437] That is to say, dire financial problems plagued colonial America, the Revolutionary War period and continued through the ratification process of the American Constitution. Early America's financial conundrum caused its economy to operate in a continued state of instability and sometimes, pandemonium.

Alexander Hamilton was appointed by President George Washington to be the first United States Secretary of the Treasury. Madison agreed with that appointment. "From the beginning (he) favored Alexander

---

[433] Ibid.
[434] Randall, p. 82.
[435] Ibid.
[436] Parry, pp. 269-270.
[437] Ketcham, p. 85.

Hamilton to head the vitally important Treasury Department."[438] Madison felt that Hamilton was the best person qualified for the position and preferred by those who had known him personally.

Hamilton understood America's monetary dilemma. In order to bring needed financial order to the nation's economy, he "never doubted the urgent need for a central bank."[439] Hamilton argued that "a central bank would provide liquid capital that would promote the ease, freedom, and efficiency of commerce."[440] In other words, the bank "could expand the money supply, extend credit to government and business, collect revenues, make debt payments, handle foreign exchange, and provide a depository for government funds."[441]

Early on, Hamilton's central bank, metaphorically, was a lightening rod of controversy. Ironically, "the opposition (to the formation of a central bank) was led by Madison" and included Jefferson and Adams.[442] These Founding Fathers became "Hamilton's three most savage critics of the 1790s."[443] They disdained banks.

Jefferson was a member of the Virginia plantation community. He scorned commerce. Jefferson held to the notion that "banks were devices to fleece the poor, oppress farmers, and induce a taste for luxury that would subvert republican simplicity."[444] "He thought that agriculture was egalitarian while manufacturing would produce a class-conscious society."[445]

Adams thought that land was the safest of investments. He "agreed in theory with Jefferson…that an agriculture society was inherently more stable than any other-not to say more virtuous."[446] Adams had strong misgivings about banks and, like many farmers, was suspicious of business and commercial interest enterprises.

These sentiments aside, Hamilton's proposal for the Bank of the United States raised the most searching question, was the Bank of the

---

[438] Ibid, p. 287.
[439] Chernow, p. 347.
[440] Ibid, p. 348.
[441] Ibid, p. 347.
[442] Kelly, p. 126.
[443] Chernow, p. 346.
[444] Ibid.
[445] Ibid.
[446] McCullough, p. 428.

United States constitutional? "This brought Madison to his feet in the House."[447]

> "He pointed out that a proposal to grant the federal government power to charter corporations like the national bank had been rejected in the Federal Convention. Furthermore, the Constitution was a 'grant of particular powers only.' Efforts to enlarge the specific powers of Congress by loose construction endangered the very notion of limited government. He then insisted that the arguments voiced in the state ratifying conventions were the proper guide in interpreting the Constitution, because in them could be found the understanding of the people of the fundamental law. In a number of conversations, Madison noted, defenders of the Constitution had denied Congress had the power to charter corporations. Furthermore, they had denied that the clause giving Congress the power to enact legislation 'necessary and proper' to effect its stated obligations, the clause upon which the national bank rested, had in any way broadened the matters on which Congress might legislate. Under this interpretation, generally accepted by federalists in 1787 and 1788, the 'necessary and proper' clause merely permitted Congress to pass laws explicitly and necessarily related to its enumerated powers."[448]

Jefferson agreed with Madison. He felt that "Hamilton was perverting the necessary-and-proper clause."[449] Jefferson "maintained that the bank bill was unconstitutional."[450]

Hamilton disagreed. He argued that the Bank of the United States was indeed constitutional. The essence of his argument "was that government must possess the means to attain ends for which it was established or the bonds of society would dissolve."[451] He went on to say "that the

---

[447] Ketcham, p. 319.
[448] Ibid, p. 320.
[449] Chernow, p. 352.
[450] Kelly, p. 126.
[451] Chernow, p. 353.

government had the right to employ all means necessary to carry out powers mentioned in the Constitution."[452] Hamilton explained that the Bank of the United States "would enable the government to make good on four powers cited explicitly in the Constitution: the rights to collect taxes, borrow money, regulate trade among states and support fleets and armies."[453] "He endorsed the dollar as the basic currency."[454] Because many Americans still bartered, he wanted the dollar denominated into smaller currency. Hamilton viewed the central bank as foundational to America's market economy.

After much heated debate, the Bank of the United States was granted a twenty-year charter by Congress on February 25, 1791. Although the bank "had 'been wisely and skillfully managed' - in 1811, President James Madison allowed the bank's charter to expire."[455] During the War of 1812 and until 1816, the persistent money problem in the United States "became a crisis of national proportions."[456] "Gold fled the country (and) merchants fell back on barter."[457] "In 1816, the Republican Congress resurrected the Bank of the United States."[458] That said, a controversial issue would carryover from the first Bank to the second Bank, and that was the question of *legality*. Was the second Bank of the United States constitutional?

In 1819, this issue was decided by the Supreme Court of the United States in a landmark case captioned *McCulloch v. Maryland*. The opinion was written by Chief Justice John Marshall. The pertinent facts in the case were these:

The state of Maryland had attempted to block operations of a branch of the second Bank of the United States located in Maryland. They did that by imposing a tax on all notes of banks not chartered in the state. Because the second Bank of the United States was the only out-of-state bank then existing in Maryland, it was quite obvious that bank had been targeted.

The Court invoked the *Necessary and Proper Clause* of the Constitution which permitted the federal government to pass laws expressly provided

---

[452] Ibid.

[453] Ibid, p. 354.

[454] Ibid, p. 356.

[455] Ibid, p. 647.

[456] Brands, H. W. *Andrew Jackson*. New York: Anchor Books, 2005, p. 332.

[457] Ibid.

[458] Ibid, p. 333.

for in the Constitution's list of expressed powers (sic). "Chief Justice Marshall's opinion became a milestone in American nationalism."[459] The decision provided for two tenets:

1. The Constitution gives Congress construed powers for effectuating the Constitution's express powers, thereby creating a national government that works (sic).
2. State action may not hinder or restrict sound constitutional exercises of power by the federal government (sic).

Chief Justice Marshall was a cousin of Jefferson's. After Marshall "upheld the constitutionality of a national bank in *McCulloch v. Maryland*, Jefferson vented his hostility to Marshall, who had asserted sweeping powers for the national government."[460] Either way, the constitutional issue regarding the second Bank of the United States had been resolved. The bank was constitutional.

The second Bank of the United States operated under the leadership of bank president Nicholas Biddle. He was a patrician, financier and politician. Biddle ran the bank until the expiration of its charter in 1836. The second bank's charter was not renewed.

In 1828, Andrew Jackson was elected seventh President of the United States. It was during his re-election campaign of 1832, that the second Bank of the United States became a central issue. Jackson held that "the basic problem with the bank was that it was unconstitutional."[461]

Bank president Biddle disagreed with Jackson's view. He, along with "the bank's defenders cited political precedent and Supreme Court decisions as providing constitutional sanction."[462] Jackson responded, "mere precedent is a dangerous source of authority, and should not be regarded as deciding questions of constitutional power except where the acquiescence of the people and the States can be considered as well settled."[463]

Jackson was re-elected president to a second term. "During the spring

[459] Morison, p. 174.
[460] Randall, p. 587.
[461] Brands, p. 469.
[462] Ibid.
[463] Ibid.

of 1833 the president prepared his anti-bank offensive carefully."[464] By October 1st, Jackson had caused federal deposits held at the Bank of the United States to be transferred to the state banks. Biddle responded, "The Bank of the United States shall not break."[465] A bank war broke out and lasted for several months. In the end, Biddle's power was crushed. He and the bank were blamed for the financial panic which resulted from the transfer of deposits from the Bank of the United States to the state banks. Jackson had successfully dismantled the second Bank of the United States.

From 1836 to 1913, the United States operated without a central bank. During that time, the country experienced ten economic recessions and six financial panics.[466] Simply put, during the seventy-seven years America operated without a Federal banking system, on average, the nation experienced either an economic downturn or monetary crisis every 4.6 years.

"Virtually every discussion of banking reform (has) commented on the frequency and severity of the United States banking crises."[467] "The desire to reduce the frequency and severity of crises-is a main point of agreement in all reform plans...that a central bank could serve as lender of last resort in a banking crisis."[468] In 1913, Congress established a regulatory agency called the Federal Reserve, "often simply called the Fed."[469] "The Fed is an example of a central bank-an institution designed to oversee the banking system and regulate the quantity of money in the economy."[470] Today, the Fed performs many of the functions envisioned by Hamilton when he established the first Bank of the United States in 1791.

The United States is a Republic.[471]

The nation operates according to laws which are consistent with the Constitution. The economic and commercial well-being of the nation relies on a central banking system which is sound. It is a fragile financial

---

[464] Ibid, p. 496.
[465] Ibid, p. 500.
[466] National Bureau of Economic Research.
[467] Meltzer, p. 68.
[468] Ibid, p. 69.
[469] Mankiw, p. 625.
[470] Ibid.
[471] The CONSTITUTION of the United States. Article. IV. Section. 4.

institution which must be managed by people who have high ethical business standards and hold to a strong moral code of conduct. Today, those values which are foundational to America's banking and financial markets system are being ignored.

The nation's polity increasingly demonstrates little regard for the importance of the tenets provided in the Constitution. This puts liberty at risk. Today, the soundness of America's banking system is on the brink of financial collapse. If the body politic doesn't restore financial integrity to its banking system and continues to have a reckless disregard for the rule of law as provided for in the Constitution, America will not survive as a Republic. If swift corrective action is not taken, the nation's economic well-being will diminish sharply and the quality of life for its citizenry will be relegated to third tier status. America will experience a lost decade, much like Japan experienced in the 1990s and the country will not maintain its status as a world leader.

CHAPTER TEN

RETURN TO FIRST PRINCIPLES

The tree of liberty must be refreshed from time to time with the blood of patriots and tyrants. It is its natural manure.

-Thomas Jefferson (1743-1826)

In the early 1960s Marxist political theory began to infiltrate the American socioeconomic and political landscape. As a result of that ingress the nation today is severely broken and it's quite possible that "All the Kings horses and all the Kings men (won't be able to) put 'Humpty Dumpty' in his place again."[472] Unless Americans are willing to take swift corrective action soon the nation could explode into a confederation, or worse. One can only speculate as to what a confederation might appear to the likes of Alice in Wonderland as she peers "through the looking-glass" and notes that the United States had been transformed into the Confederation of North America.[473]

Under some pretext such as the Texas-American Annexation Treaty of 1848, Alice discovers Texas was the first state to secede from the *Union*. Joined by Oklahoma, these two states formed Region No.1. Immediately thereafter, nine of the eleven "Confederate States of America" (ca 1860-1865) were joined by Kentucky and West Virginia and formed Region No. 2. To consolidate power, the Marxists formed Region No. 3 which included Maine, New England, New York and the Mid-Atlantic states.

---

[472] Carroll, Lewis. *Through the Looking-Glass and What Alice Found There.* New York: Barnes & Noble Classics, 2004, p. 215.

[473] Ibid, p. 145.

Because of the federal government's takeover of the automobile industry, Ohio and Michigan were annexed to Region No.3.

Alaska stood alone as Region No. 4. The states in Region No. 5 were essentially the mid-western states which included: Indiana, Illinois, Wisconsin, Minnesota, North Dakota, South Dakota, Iowa, Missouri, Kansas and Nebraska. Region No. 6 was comprised of: Colorado, Wyoming, Montana, Utah, Idaho and Nevada. Oregon and Washington State formed Region No. 7. The last region to develop was Region 8 which included: California, Arizona, New Mexico and Hawaii. That left Florida. The northern one-third of the state was sympathetic to Region No. 2, while the Atlantic coast side was desirous of being a part of Region No. 3 and the Gulf coast side of the state held preference to be included with Region No. 5. Sadly, Florida dissolved.

Would Alice find such a patchwork of competing forces of counter-productivity entertaining?

Because of their dominance in energy and food distribution; like a Hobbsian *Leviathan*, Regions 1, 4 and 5 formed a *Tricor*. This simile became the central governing power for all the Confederation of North America. Washington, DC was absorbed by Region No. 2 and became that region's capitol. It continued to provide a number of government services to the confederation on a contract basis; region by region. For the most part however, the former District of Columbia became merely a symbol of an earlier historic period now long past.

No patriotic American is desirous of having the United States become a confederation. As Huntington points out, "confederations don't last long" and what would come after the Confederation of North America would be Armageddon.[474]

Over the past forty-five years, Marxist elements have crept into American society and have put the nation on the brink of collapse.

Today, Americans face an exigency in health care.[475] The nation is experiencing the worst financial calamity since the Great Depression of the 1930s. This has caused personal financial security and independence

---

[474] Huntington, p. 19.
[475] Appendix G.

for a large number of Americans to be in near ruin.[476] Personal safety in the United States is at crisis levels. Every day in America, 65 people are killed and more than 6,000 are wounded in interpersonal violence.

If America's citizenry fail to come to terms with the looming socioeconomic and political crucial period soon, an inevitable rebellion will take place in the United States. This rebellion will have much bloodshed. It is critical to derail anarchy now.

The body politic must mobilize independently led 'Movements.'

The goal is to restore the nation to its goodness by returning to First Principles. These principles were established by *The Founders* and are those tenets which made America great in the first place.

America's civil society is in need of repair.

A first step is for the American family of the 21st century to be retooled. Old fashioned parent nurturing and supervision need to be reinstated into that venerable institution. Because of financial demands on today's young families, the dual-earner-dual-carer paradigm has become more common and quite challenging. For those families desirous of having a stay-at-home parent, the American tax code needs to be revised to provide tax incentives to accommodate that arrangement. The legislature has taken a first step in this direction by enacting "laws like the Family Medical Leave Act of 1993."[477] These kinds of programs need to be expanded. The legislature needs to devise methods of compensation to recognize this fact and make these modern day family arrangements work. *Latch-key kids*, especially middle school and teenagers who come home from school to an 'empty nest', are placed at high risk. Equally kids who are nurtured at sterile Platonic day-care centers do not fare much better. Tomorrow's citizens deserve much better and the first place to start is in nurturing a positive home environment.

Educational reform is mandatory for the nation to begin to return to First Principles. Public schools as well as state colleges and universities must draft a Code of Ethics. This code, among other things, would require teachers and college instructors to abandon all didactic use of *political*

---

[476] *USA Today.* <u>For Boomers, Recession is Redefining Retirement</u>. June 17, 2009.
[477] Bazelon, Emily. <u>The Place of Women on the Court</u>. New York: *The New York Times Magazine.* July 12, 2009, p. 47.

correctness in their teaching methodologies and in its place, teach students responsible speech. Responsible speech is respectful speech without the tyrannical overtones of political correctness.

Parents must demand from their local public school administrators the right to have representation on school curriculum and textbook selection committees. This will provide a third party look to ensure that schools are selecting balanced textbooks to enrich student's learning experience. It will help to ensure course presentations are being made in accordance with the approved class syllabus. It will provide a system of checks and balances so that teachers do not stray from their course outlines and promote their personal socioeconomic and political agendas in the classroom.

Today, nearly all schools have a mandatory class involving sex education. What most schools don't have is a course telling students of the unintended consequences if they experiment with what was learned in that classroom with a fellow classmate of the opposite sex. In other words, students are often not taught that such experimentation may well lead to an unplanned teen pregnancy. In addition to sex education, all schools must develop a course entitled *Parenting*. Here, students will be taught, among other things, the responsibility that goes with being a parent. The curriculum will address the financial obligations associated with parenting and the demands associated with raising a child.

Finally, high schools must make a course in *Civics* mandatory for graduation. Students will be taught how the government is organized and operates in a Republic. America has evolved into an ever increasing litigious society. It is important that students learn how the court appointment and election process for judges work. They must come to understand that in addition to legal experience, court appointees often bring to the bench their "life experiences" as well. This impacts the way they decide cases.[478] It is critical that judges come to rely not on personal life experiences, but hold fast to the stricture of the Constitution when deciding cases. Life experiences wire people in obscure ways. That is to say, a judge's perception of a particular event involving a case they are ruling could well be wrong. If a misguided perception were to be factored into a court decision it will result in bad case law. This in turn will have an adverse and lasting impact on civil society. Students one day

---

[478] Ibid, pp. 24 and 47.

will become adults. It is critical that they learn early the importance of executive appointments and as citizens be prepared to engage fully the court appointment process.

Again, Machiavelli cautions that "For the generality of men feed on what appears as much as on what is; indeed, many times they are moved more by things that appear than by things that are."[479] It is a truism that perception is reality. It is important that judges get it right the first time. By staying close to the Constitution the risk of error is minimized.

The nation's financial system needs to be rebuilt.

It wasn't *Capitalism* that caused the financial meltdown and economic collapse of the early 21st century in America. It was the <u>abuse</u> of *Capitalism* that was responsible for this calamity. During the Reagan Administration in the early 1980s, Keynesianism had been replaced by Libertarianism as an economic theory. The present financial debacle was brought about by the actions of greedy Wall Street bankers and brazen real estate promoters who utilized unregulated and leveraged high-risk OTC swap and derivative products to achieve their trading objectives.

The federal government must take swift action and launch a formal investigation in the trading of OTC swap and derivative products by banks and brokerage firms who, as of September 2008, have been identified as having major positions of these toxic products on their balance sheets. As a part of the investigation, officials should perform a Trade Practice Analysis on each financial institution identified that would include:

* Matching critical buy and sell trades.
* Following the money flows among the institutions being investigated.
* Identifying the counterparties to swap and derivative trades which are a part of the examination.
* Determining the locations of profitable trades.
* Concluding as to whether or not customers' positions were compromised as a result of the banks or brokerage firms trading in their proprietary accounts.

If it is discovered that any laws were violated, federal government

---

[479] Machiavelli, p. 60.

officials must take swift legal action against identified firm(s) and their officers.

Congress must reinstate the Glass-Steagall Act of 1933. As the Federal Reserve structure is overhauled, the position of Chairman should be abolished and replaced with a Supervisory Board. The board membership should rotate every four years on a staggered regional basis.

The majority of banks in the United States are financially sound. Only a handful of large money-center banks are insolvent. Their balance sheets are filled with worthless derivative instruments that for all intents and purposes will probably never regain value. A Two Tier banking system needs to be structured. Sound banks would operate on Tier One and problematic banks would operate on Tier Two. The too big to fail concept is passé. Problematic banks would have one year to regain sound financial footing. If they are unable to meet this requirement, they will be allowed to fail quietly.

The federal government should ban the trading of OTC derivative and swap products now and shut that market down.

Nicole Bullock is a columnist for the *Financial Times*. In an article entitled US munis face 'growing credit risk', she explains just how pathetic these financial instruments really are. Bullock illustrates how municipalities use variable rate demand obligations, or VRDOs, "to pay low short-term interest rates, despite the need for long-term financing."[480] The problem is the derivatives that typically accompany VRDOs. "These are interest rate swaps that allow a municipality to exchange the payment of a floating rate for a fixed income rate."[481] Many swaps were set during the period of high interest rates. Now that interest rates have fallen, many municipalities are 'out of the money.' The exit fee to unwind these losing transactions is unconscionable. Bullock says, "The interest rate rises potentially by five times or more, and the issuer has to repay the bonds in four to six years instead of 25 to 30 years."[482] This causes municipalities to now replace VRDOs with more expensive fixed rate debt and places further stress on the balance sheets of banks who acted as buyers of last resort. Congress

---

[480] Bullock, Nicole. US munis face 'growing credit risk'. *Financial Times*. Wednesday, December 15, 2010, p. 22.
[481] Ibid.
[482] Ibid.

can no longer allow this market to operate. The evidence is overwhelming. The OTC swap and derivative market is nothing more than *Three Card Monty*. Congress must shut this market down now!

Given the evidence to date, derivative products have had a near twenty-year track record that has been nothing short of an unmitigated disaster. These derivative products are ineffective as a risk management tool. They serve no economic purpose whatsoever. Congress must move quickly. To do nothing is tantamount to dereliction of duty and amounts to a gross breach of the public trust.

In order to restore integrity to the dollar and help stabilize the international monetary system United States debt obligations should be monetized with *Gold*. In so doing, this action would help reduce volatility in the global foreign exchange and crude oil markets.

Political Calamity in America.

The current economic crisis in the United States has caused a certain transparency to emerge which reveals a hybrid political theory developing on the nation's business and political landscape. This newly contrived theory, herein called "Duoism" has been evolving from an activist Progressive-Socialist and Libertarian ideology which has been developing in the United States for nearly half a century. This so-called *Duoism* is a radical departure from the concept of a Republic as understood by the nation's *Founders* and the Capitalistic paradigm of Adam Smith which followed. Duoism operates as a totalitarian regime and is governed by a dictator.

Freddie Mac and Fannie Mae represent *Duoism* in action.

Duoism is an incestuous alliance between the federal government and certain major American corporations. Its operations are corrupt and ultimately lead to the destruction of the nation. The "Duocracy" begins to take shape as more and more of America's corporate executives abandon their social responsibilities to employees and the nation, and begin to focus all their energy solely on making money. These corporate titans begin to look increasingly for ways to joint-venture with the United States federal government and host governments abroad for the sole purpose of acquiring massive amounts of personal wealth and power. They are an oligarchy.

An early sign that a company's executives are desirous of a Duocratic arrangement is to have the federal government take over certain responsibilities such as the administration of their employee health care and pension plans. This enables them to roam the globe seeking enhanced corporate profit and executive bonus enrichment. As pointed out earlier, Naomi Klein noted that American multinational organizations often establish "factories (that) are cheaply constructed and tossed together on land that is rented, not owned."[483] She continued by saying that these factories are typically located in "... tax-free areas (situated in) third world economies (and employ) cheap, non-union workforce assemblies (where) the vast majority of workers are women."[484] According to this *Business Plan*, the American workforce is abandoned and replaced by cheap labor abroad. The sole purpose is to enhance year-end bonuses for the oligarchial elite who run these multi-national corporations. These lost jobs will probably never return to the United States.

The emerging Duocracy's organizational structure is ultimately *totalitarian*. The goal of the "Duoistic Alliance" is power and influence. In other words, the United States federal government provides influence on foreign regimes (making countries do what America wants them to do) which in turn paves the way to facilitate American business interest in the global economy. Political correctness is interwoven in all communication procedures. Duocracy's nature is *cosmopolitanism*. Its enemy is nationalism. On the *Isms* Matrix, Duoism would be positioned to the right of Communism and left center of Nazism and Fascism. It is best described as an elitist oligarchy governed by a *Totalitarian* leader.

The tools the Progressive Socialist elites use to achieve their goal of *Totalitarian* governance include: 1) the destruction of the American family unit, 2) reducing religion to irrelevancy, 3) a takeover of American industry and the banking system and 4) making clever use of political correctness in the media and school classrooms. This allows the Progressives to gain power over the body politic and readily engineer a society of conformists. Their political tactics include making *ad hominem* attacks on their political opponents, engage in telling lies about their opposition and conduct character assassination against innocent people including children. This communication tactic is taken directly from the Nazi and Communist playbooks.

---

[483] Klein, *No Logo*, p. 206.
[484] Ibid, pp. 204-205 and 207.

The Duoists goal is to gain *power* and *control* over the American people and confiscate their personal assets. Their objective is to deny a person's right to bear arms. The Duocratic-Progressive elite want to confiscate peoples' guns. Milestones to achieve their objectives include the: 1) confiscation of people's private property, 2) enactment of adverse laws and 3) aggressive use of costly litigation and court actions.

To illustrate, in July 2009, a column appeared in the *Wall Street Journal* which reported that Alaska Governor Sarah Palin announced she would step down July 26, 2009 as Governor.[485] Palin had faced 16 ethics inquiries of one sort or another in Alaska since 2008, the Wall Street Journal reported. Lt. Governor Sean Parnell said at the time "that her (Palin's) decision (to step down) was primarily prompted by her concern over $2 million a year the state has spent on records requests and the ethics inquiries." He said, "I think she used the word 'insane' in describing those costs."[486] Regardless of one's political conviction in either support of, or opposition to Sarah Palin, all well-intentioned Americans should be outraged at the litigation tactics which were used to drive this woman from public office.

Litigation is the most popular tool in the Progressive toolbox and is most detrimental to the well-being of the United States. If the Progressive elite are allowed to continue the use of Nazi like behavior using political correctness, frivolous lawsuits and other forms of intimidation to foster their political agenda, it will destroy the nation for good. There will be no turning back without much bloodshed. If America is to survive as a Republic, the Progressive-Socialist influence must be removed permanently from the American political landscape. If that influence is left in tact, America runs a serious risk of tyrannical rule.

Who are these Duocratic elites? What are their names? How can they be identified? Where do they live? There is not a readily available roster of their names. Their identity is obscure. The simile is that the Duocratic Progressive-Socialist elites operate on a political landscape much like Adam Smith's *invisible hand* operates on the economic frontier.[487]

They are identified in large part by their rhetoric and actions. They are people who support the twelve tenets of the Communist Manifesto.[488]

---

[485] *The Wall Street Journal.* July 6, 2009.
[486] Ibid.
[487] Smith, p. xviii.
[488] Marx, pp. 26-28.

These Marxist Progressives operate in many villages, towns and cities in the nation. Their numbers are small, but their effectiveness has been impressive. Marxism is operative right now in the United States and has been for more than half a century. It must be brought to an end now; otherwise the liberty of every American is in jeopardy.

The question is can anything really be done to stop Duocratic Totalitarianism and derail an imploding Rebellion in America? The answer is a resounding 'Yes'-but time is running out. There is only one way this malignant cancer can be stopped from spreading further and destroying American civil society and that is for the nation to confront this evil *head-on*. Here's how it would work.

Return to First Principles.

First, to bring about a halt to the further spread of this phenomenon, Totalitarian Duoism in American society, there has to be a fundamental understanding of the problem and its resulting consequences.

> **The nation *must come to an agreement that the solution to the problem lies in a return to First Principles as established by* The Founders.**

Targets for this national understanding are the forty percent of civil society who claim to be independent of any political party affiliation. In common they cherish liberty, hold to the notion that private property is central to a Republic; they are patriotic and champion nationalism. Regarding nationalism, Schlesinger points out that "after two centuries *nationalism* remains the most vital political emotion in the world-far more vital than social ideologies such as communism or fascism or even democracy."[489]

Continuing, these Americans look to the Revolutionary War as a defining moment in America's history. They view that event with pride and as being central to the founding of the Republic. These patriots hold that the Constitution is unwavering and serves as the nation's governing legal document.

Today, "Independents" comprise nearly forty percent of the voting block in America.[490] They are everyone's neighbor and co-worker. They

---

[489] Schlesinger, p. 53.
[490] www.independentvoting.org.

are plumbers, carpenters, electricians, brick layers, painters and auto mechanics who build things and make things work. They are barbers and hairdressers. They are secretaries, computer technicians, nurses and memorable third-grade school teachers. They are coal miners and farmers. Sadly, they are the hundreds of thousands of near forgotten factory workers in America. They are cab drivers, bus drivers, truck drivers and railroad workers. They are the countless other occupations too numerous to list here, but that's who 'they' are. Most importantly, they are the women and men of all the nation's armed forces. These Americans risk their lives daily so that others may live in peace and freedom. That's where the national understanding will originate. This is where the *Movements* will gain traction in guiding the nation toward a return to First Principles.

The Movements are **not** an amalgamation of *ad hoc* third political parties. The Movements are an *idea* about America in the 21st century and how its citizenry will be able to continue living in a Republic. The Movements are about preserving the American family, retaining jobs in the United States, protecting the historical importance of the Judea-Christian influence on American culture and restoring ethics in business and government. Most important, the Movements hold to the notion of *The Founders* that the Constitution is a sacred document which provides a foundation for First Principles of America.

All too often "our government has not only been partial in matters of socioeconomic and political dynamics; but those also who have suffered under that partiality, and have therefore endeavoured by their writings (and actions) to vindicate their own rights and liberties, have for the most part done it upon narrow principles, suited only to the interests of their own sects."[491] The majority of Americans have suffered under the divisiveness and partiality of the Duocratic Progressive Movement. This is evident given the condition of America's: 1) family unit, 2) educational system, 3) manufacturing and factory assembly plant workforce, 4) banking system and 5) economy. This is no longer acceptable and no longer can the Progressive Socialists be ignored. No longer can the Marxist agenda in America be denied. No longer can the socialist agenda be tolerated in America.

The Movements must engage the Duocracy directly. A reverse "Cloward-Piven strategy of forcing political change through orchestrated

---

[491] Locke, p. 114.

crisis" must be considered.[492] The Marxists in America are small in number. They make noise and draw attention to their political agenda. They lampoon their opposition and are a formidable enemy. They are well financed and have over forty-five years of successful experience in planting the destructive seeds of totalitarianism in American society. On the other hand they are shallow in character and weak in nature. When confronted with strong opposing conviction, they buckle.

The "strategy in dealing with disharmony" is to understand that "knowledge of the problem is key to the solution." The "peak efficiency of knowledge and strategy is to make conflict altogether unnecessary."[493] If Americans fail to gain true knowledge of the problem and are unable to develop a consensus as to a workable strategy to derail the Marxist-Socialist ideology from their agenda, then the nation will heighten the risk of dealing with a very bloody Rebellion.

The Movements are not about gathering for mass rallies and drawing media attention to a cause. The Movements are about the gathering of like-minded people in small groups of ten or less. This is a natural place to begin. Putnam notes that "Visiting with friends and acquaintances has long been one of the most important social practices in America."[494] It is in this setting that based on individual community and state dynamics, quality discourse takes place, workable action plans are developed and implementation procedures are devised. Later, when people do gather in larger group settings they will be able to share with one another knowledge and strategies arrived at in earlier hometown small group gatherings.

Among other things, strategy discussions should include how to: 1) actively engage the Duocratic Progressive Socialists in court actions, 2) consider the calling for a 'Constitutional Convention,' 3) expand the use of the *impeachment* process, 4) identify and use 'power' groups who share the same political philosophy of the Movements and 5) be prepared to 'take to the streets' and plan for "non-violent civil disobedience" to remove the oligarchial elite from the socioeconomic and political landscape in America.[495]

---

[492] www.sterlingtimes.com.
[493] Sun Tzu. *The Art of War*. London: Shambhala Publications, Inc., 1991, p. xi.
[494] Putnam, p. 95.
[495] www.theKingcenter.org.

American society must remove corrupt
officials from *Government* service

Topics for discussion in small group settings include: 1) ballot-box reform, 2) term limits; (a) six years for the President, (b) three terms maximum for Congress, (c) Senate and House Committee memberships to rotate every four years and (d) cumulative term limits of fifteen years for judges, 3) legal procedures to remove corrupt judges from the bench, 4) enforcement of the law, 5) punishment, 6) holding government officials accountable, 7) calling for all businesses to write a *Code of Ethics* which, among other things, would address the moral responsibilities businesses have to communities in which they operate, 8) stewardship, 9) civic mindedness and 10) developing the *public will* to return to First Principles which formed America.[496]

The Movements are aimed at furthering an independent political constituency in America. In his text *By Invitation Only*, Steven Schier describes "activation" as meaning "the more contemporary methods that parties, interest groups, and candidates employ to induce particular, finely targeted portions of the public to become active in elections, demonstrations, and lobbying." He concludes that it was activation (the mass use of special interest groups) which "destroyed the prospects for majority rule in American politics."[497] The Movements are anchored in Independent political theory. Logocentric to that theory is the idea of *majority rule* in American civil society. The tenets of Independent political theory are described in George Washington's Farewell Address (Appendix B) and Thomas Jefferson's First Inaugural Address (Appendix C).[498]

The Movements will galvanize an overwhelming force which will crush the Progressive Movement and reduce it to irrelevancy. The Movements will ensure all Americans the promise *The Founders* made over two hundred years ago. Thus, America will continue to be a nation where all its citizenry may reside in peace, liberty, happiness and prosperity. Most important, the Movements will remove the threat of the United States ever becoming a totalitarian Duocracy.

---

[496] Appendix J
[497] Schier, pp. 7 and 9.
[498] Appendices B and C.

CHAPTER ELEVEN

CONCLUSION

The Constitution of the United States was made not merely for the generation that then existed, but for posterity-unlimited, undefined, endless, perpetual posterity.
-Henry Clay (1777-1852)

Historian Bernard Bailyn noted that "from 1500 to the present" there was a transformation of people away from their original center of habitation-a movement of people to the Western Hemisphere.[499] Bailyn calls this event "the peopling of the North American continent and argues "it forms the foundation of American history."[500] He continues by saying that "The Peopling of British North America ...brings together the major aspects of life in the American colonies (which includes:) 1) social structure and settlement patterns, 2) demography and politics, 3) agriculture and religion, 4) mobility, 5) family organizations, and 6) ethnic relations."[501] In other words it "places the whole evolving story of American life within the broadest possible context of Western history."[502]

Bailyn notes that "pamphlets (were) the distinctive literature of the (American) Revolution" and after much study of those literary works concluded "that the American Revolution was above all else an ideological, constitutional, political struggle and not primarily a controversy between social groups undertaken to force change in the

---

[499] Bernard Bailyn is an American historian, author and professor at Harvard University.
[500] Bailyn, *The Peopling of British North America*, pp. 4-5.
[501] Ibid, p. 7.
[502] Ibid.

organization of the society or the economy." He argues that "the primary goal of the American Revolution ... was not the overthrow or even the alteration of the existing social order but the preservation of political liberty threatened by the apparent corruption of the unwritten British constitution, and the establishment in principle of the existing conditions of liberty."[503]

The War of Independence was fought during the period 1775-1783. America emerged victorious from this conflict. "The Revolution furnished Americans an opportunity to give *legal* form to their political ideals."[504] On May 25, 1787 a Federal Convention opened in Philadelphia "for the sole and express purpose of revising the Articles of Confederation, to render the federal constitution adequate to the exigencies of government, and the preservation of the Union."[505] It is here that "we see the germ of the doctrine that the Constitution is *supreme law,* that acts contrary to it are *void,* and that the courts are the proper agents to enforce it."[506]

With the Constitution now ratified the former commander of the Continental Army, General George Washington, looked forward to the quiet seclusion of his farm in Virginia. Washington had achieved his "most important contribution to the American Constitution" and that was his "strong commitment to civilian control of the military."[507] "But voices from all directions were calling for his continued leadership."[508] In 1789 George Washington was elected to serve as the nation's first President and John Adams was elected the nation's first Vice President.

Washington and Adams would serve two terms as President and Vice President respectively. Washington's second term was turbulent. Central to this disturbance was a growing schism between Alexander Hamilton, Washington's appointee to head the *US Treasury* and Thomas Jefferson, Washington's *Secretary of State.*

"Hamilton wished to concentrate power; Jefferson, to diffuse it. Hamilton feared anarchy and cherished order; Jefferson feared tyranny and cherished liberty. Hamilton believed republican government could only succeed if directed by a governing class; Jefferson, that republicanism

[503] Bailyn, *The Ideological Origins of the American Revolution,* pp. x, 8 and 19.
[504] Morison, p. 97.
[505] Ibid, p. 114.
[506] Ibid, p. 116.
[507] Bowling, Kenneth R. *The Founding Fathers and the Society of the Cincinnati.* Washington, DC: Symposium at the auditorium of The Phillips Collection, September 19, 2008.
[508] Parry, p. 507.

required a democratic base. Hamilton took the gloomy Hobbesian view of human nature; Jefferson, a more hopeful view: the people, he believed, were the safest and most virtuous, though not always the wisest depository of power; education would perfect their wisdom. All those differences were bracketed by two opposed conceptions of what America was and might be."[509] The irony is how Hamilton and Jefferson found commonality in their idea for America, but yet were so divergent and extreme in their methodology as to how that idea should be administered governmentally.

Over time people began to grow sympathetic to one of the two political theories. "Jefferson's followers called themselves *Republicans* and Hamilton's followers called themselves *Federalists*. That division proved to be the birth of political parties in the United States."[510] Jefferson "would later write, 'If I could not go to heaven but with a party, I would not go there at all'."[511]

The year 1794 "witnessed a marked acceleration in the trend toward the emergence of two national parties, a development which almost everyone viewed with dismay."[512] Each party thought the other to be treacherous. The logic was grounded in the notion that "in a well-ordered society there could be no place for a party system" and George Washington agreed.[513]

On September 17, 1796 President George Washington described his political experience in a farewell address to his fellow Americans. Central to his presentation was a call for union and a warning about "the dangers of parties in the State." Specifically this is what Washington had to say on the matter:

> "I have already intimated to you the danger of parties in the State, with particular reference to the founding of them on geographical discriminations. Let me now take a more comprehensive view, and warn you in the most solemn manner against the baneful effects of the spirit of party generally.

---

[509] Morison, p. 131.
[510] Parry, p. 552.
[511] Morison, p. 131.
[512] Ibid, p. 135.
[513] Ibid.

This spirit, unfortunately, is inseparable from our nature, having its root in the strongest passions of the human mind. It exists under different shapes in all governments, more or less stifled, controlled, or repressed; but, in those of the popular form, it is seen in its greatest rankness, and is truly their worst enemy.

The alternate domination of one faction over another, sharpened by the spirit of revenge, natural to party dissension, which in different ages and countries has perpetrated the most horrid enormities, is itself a frightful *despotism*. But this leads at length to a more formal and permanent despotism. The disorders and miseries which result gradually incline the minds of men to seek security and repose in the absolute power of an individual; and sooner or later the chief of some prevailing faction, more able or more fortunate than his competitors, turns this disposition to the purposes of his own elevation, in the ruins of public liberty.

Without looking forward to an extremity of this kind (which nevertheless ought not to be entirely out of sight), the common and continual mischiefs of the spirit of party are sufficient to make it the interest and duty of a wise people to discourage and restrain it."[514]

Turning to the role the Constitution was to play in the forming and sustaining of America, Bailyn argues "The ideological history of the American Revolution developed in three distinct phases."[515] They were the: 1) development of political thought and sets of ideas, 2) crafting of state constitutions and 3) finalization of the national constitution."[516] Washington held steadfast to the notion that the Constitution was the epicenter of the new Republic. In his Farewell Address he explained his views by saying:

"Profoundly penetrated with this idea, I shall carry it with me to my grave, as a strong indictment to unceasing vows

---

[514] Appendix B.
[515] Bailyn, *The Ideological Origins of the American Revolution*, pp. 323-324.
[516] Ibid.

that heaven may continue to you the choicest tokens of its beneficence; that your union and brotherly affection may be perpetual; that the free **Constitution**, which is the work of your hands, may be sacredly maintained; that its administration in every department may be stamped with wisdom and virtue; that, in fine, the happiness of the people of these States, under the auspices of liberty, may be made complete by so careful a preservation and so prudent a use of this blessing as will acquire to them the glory of recommending it to the applause, the affection, and adoption of every nation which is yet a stranger to it.

The basis of our political systems is the right of the people to make and to alter their constitutions of government. But the **Constitution** which at any time exists, till changed by an explicit and authentic act of the whole people, is sacredly obligatory upon all. The very idea of the power and the right of the people to establish government presupposes the duty of every individual to obey the established government.

Towards the preservation of your government, and the permanency of your present happy state, it is requisite, not only that you steadily discountenance irregular oppositions to its acknowledged authority, but also that you resist with care the spirit of innovation upon its principles, however specious the pretexts. One method of assault may be to effect, in the forms of the **Constitution**, alterations which will impair the energy of the system, and thus to undermine what cannot be directly overthrown. If in the opinion of the people, the distribution or modification of the constitutional powers be in any particular wrong, let it be corrected by an amendment in the way which the **Constitution** designates. But let there be no change by usurpation; for though this, in one instance, may be the instrument of good, it is the customary weapon by which free governments are destroyed. The precedent must always greatly overbalance in permanent evil any partial or transient benefit, which the use can at any time yield."[517]

Thomas Jefferson followed George Washington and John Adams as the third President of the United States. In his First Inaugural Address given on March 4, 1801 Jefferson, like Washington, made reference to the **Constitution**.

> "Utterly, indeed, should I despair did not the presence of many whom I here see remind me that in the other high authorities provided by our **Constitution** I shall find resource of wisdom, of virtue, and of zeal on which to rely under all difficulties. To you, then, gentlemen, who are charged with the sovereign functions of legislation, and to those associated with you, I look with encouragement for that guidance and support which may enable us to steer with safety the vessel in which we are all embarked amidst the conflicting elements of a troubled world.
>
> During the contest of opinion through which we have passed the animation of discussions and of exertions has sometimes worn an aspect which might impose on strangers unused to think freely and to speak and to write what they think; but this being now decided by the voice of the nation, announced according to the rules of the **Constitution**, all will, of course, arrange themselves under the will of the law, and united in common efforts for the common good. All, too, will bear in mind this sacred principle, that though **the will of the majority is in all cases to prevail**, that will to be rightful must be reasonable; that the minority posses their equal rights, which equal law must protect, and to violate would be oppression."[518]

Jefferson and Washington viewed the Constitution as a revered document. Both men felt the Constitution was a document complete with

---

[517] Appendix B.
[518] Appendix C.

wisdom and virtue. Washington held to the notion that the Constitution was a legal document for all the citizenry to obey and changes could only be made by the people through the amendment process. Jefferson held that the Constitution provided guidance to all those charged with the sovereign functions of legislation operating in a troubled world.

Washington and Jefferson are the two key actors whose professional careers illustrate accurately the prevailing conditions during colonial and post-colonial America. These men are the preeminent figures among the *Founding Fathers*. Their philosophies, ideas and political theories about America provide a clear roadmap as to how best the nation can return to First Principles.

Central to what that idea of America should be, the colonists held to the notion of "the natural rights (of man) philosophy" and that American principles must be "embodied in constitutional practice."[519] They embraced the "sanctity of private property" and held that "institutions were remodeled and laws altered in accordance with advanced doctrine on the nature of liberty."[520]

Fundamental to the colonists was the "populist cry against corruption."[521]

There is another dimension to the founding of America which lies with the countless number of women and men of all stripes who fought for America's independence. Were it not for their sacrifice of "blood, sweat and tears," the framers such as Washington and Jefferson would have had little upon which to build the United States.[522] Who were these people? What were they seeking? Where did they live? Why were these obscure personalities so willing to sacrifice their lives just for an idea?

"Crispus Attucks, a former slave, was living in Boston on March 5, 1770. Hearing of a fight between some citizens of Boston and British soldiers, Attucks boldly took the lead at the front of the crowd and struck one of the British soldiers. The soldier fired and hit Attucks with two musket balls. Four other men were killed and six were mortally wounded."[523]

---

[519] Bailyn, Bernard. *Faces of Revolution*. New York: Vintage Books, 1992, pp. 201 and 203.
[520] Ibid, pp. 191 and 206.
[521] Ibid, pp. 204-205.
[522] Churchill, Winston. *Blood, Sweat and Tears*. May 13, 1940.
[523] Beier, Anne. *Crispus Attucks: Hero of the Boston Massacre*. New York: Rosen Publishing Group, 2003, cover jacket.

Joseph Plumb Martin was born on Thanksgiving Day 1760 in Berkshire County, Massachusetts. Both his grandparents were farmers. When he was seven years old Martin was sent to live with his mother's father in Connecticut. He remained there until he was fifteen years old. On July 16, 1776 Martin enlisted in the Continental Army and served for the duration of the war. Martin kept copious notes of his adventures. These accounts were archived in a literary text which would later serve as a primary source document for historical research.[524]

Haym Salomon operated a successful brokerage business in Philadelphia. "He was by birth and rearing a Polish Jew."[525] Salomon was devout and embraced a deep hatred of tyranny. "There is a story, strongly supported by anecdotal evidence, that he once violated the letter of Jewish law to serve the cause of freedom that he believed sacred."[526]

> "It was Yom Kippur, a holy day when financial transactions were forbidden. A messenger from Robert Morris (Philadelphia businessman and committee member of the Continental Congress) came to the door of the synagogue while a worship service was in progress. Funds were needed immediately to keep Washington's army in the field. While Morris's man waited, Salomon solicited the congregation and, personally adding to their contributions, provided the necessary thousands of dollars."[527]

In Massachusetts, Deborah Sampson took the name "Robert Shurtliff" and served as a Continental soldier during the Revolutionary war. "She did not rebel against a 'contracted' female sphere, ... Yet she linked her personal quest with the nation's quest for 'FREEDOM and INDEPENDENCE' as did countless other people in the Revolutionary era. To magnify the importance of her enlistment, she exaggerated the low state of the American cause. 'And whilst poverty, hunger, nakedness, cold and diseases had dwindled the American armies to a handful,' while

[524] Roop, Connie and Peter. *The Diary of Joseph Plumb Martin, a Revolutionary War Soldier.* Tarrytown: Benchmark Books, 2001, pp. 7-11.
[525] Mapp, Jr., Alf J. *The Faiths of Our Fathers.* New York: Fall River Press, 2006, p. 146.
[526] Ibid.
[527] Ibid, p. 150.

' even *Washington* himself' was 'tottering over the abyss of destruction,' she decided to 'throw off the soft habiliments of *my sex* and assume those of the *warrior*.'"[528]

Julius Rutherford enlisted in the Continental Army in 1776 for a three year term. He was assigned to the 2nd Battalion of the 12th Virginia Regiment commanded by Colonel James Wood, son of Mary Rutherford Wood. He fought in the Battle of Brandywine and numerous other skirmishes. He was honorably discharged in 1779. His pension application was approved and beginning on July 4, 1818 he received a pension in the amount of $8 per month. "In 1828, he was by reason of his age and infirmity, totally unable to provide for himself and his family, as he was crippled in his right hip while in the army, by a horse falling through a bridge on him. One of his arms had 'perished away' and the other is 'in a measure withering' so as to render him helpless."[529] Julius Rutherford, the Revolutionary War soldier, died in Anderson County, Tennessee, on May 17, 1839.

These five actors portray an image of the post-colonial period which is symbolic of the idea of America. This landscape however, is rapidly becoming unraveled. The principles forged by these five colonists and the thousands of others like them are rapidly disappearing. Unless the people of the United States return to First Principles, for them, America will be "agony in stony places." Metaphorically, the nation will be a place of "Falling towers, empty chapel(s)" and buildings that have "no windows." The country will have become a perdurable *Waste Land*.[530]

In his text *Who Are We?* Huntington points out that "Americans ... are defined and united by their commitment to the political principles of liberty, equality, democracy, individualism, human rights, the rule of law, and private property embodied in the American Creed."[531] He observes that "The political ideas of the American Creed have been the basis of national identity."[532] Huntington noted that America's body politic was comprised first of settlers who were of Anglo-Protestant ethnicity followed by immigrants from numerous other lands. George Washington

---

[528] Young, Alfred F. *Masquerade*. New York: Vintage Books, 2004, pp. 4 and 221.

[529] Kegley, Mary B. *Early Adventures on the Western Waters*. Volume III, Part 2. Marceline: Walsworth Publishing Company, 1995, pp. 500-501.

[530] Eliot, T.S. *The Waste Land and Other Poems*. New York: Harcourt, Brace & World, Inc., 1934, pp. 42 and 44.

[531] Huntington, p. 46. Schlesinger, pp. 33 and 37. Appendix D.

[532] Huntington, p. 46

provided strict guidance to immigrants entering America. Washington said:

> "'The bosom of America is open ... to the oppressed and persecuted of all Nations and Religions.' But he counseled newcomers against retaining the 'Language, habits and principles (good or bad) which they bring with them.' Let them come not in clannish groups but as individuals, prepared for 'intermixture with our people.' Then they would be 'assimilated to our customs, measures and laws: in a word, soon become *one people.*'"[533]

John Quincy Adams "insisted on the distinctness of the new American identity. When a German baron contemplating emigration interviewed Adams as secretary of state, Adams admonished his visitor that immigrants had to make up their mind to one thing:"

> 'They must cast off the European skin, never to resume it. They must look forward to their posterity rather than backward to the ancestors.'[534]

Huntington argues, that "the Anglo-Protestant culture of their settler forebears survived for three hundred years as the paramount defining element of American identity."[535] That is to say as immigrants came to America, they seemed to shed their cultural heritage and were desirous of adopting the 'settler paradigm.' With the message came the symbol – *I am an American.*

Huntington sees a dangerous emergence in 21st century America. He envisions a "cosmopolitan and imperialist attempt to eliminate social, political and cultural differences between America and other societies."[536] *Cosmopolitanism* is rooted in The Frankfurt School. Its underpinnings are Marxist and the goal is to destroy America. Huntington holds that "The alternative to cosmopolitanism and imperialism is *nationalism* devoted to the preservation and enhancement of those qualities that have defined

---

[533] Schlesinger, p. 30.
[534] Ibid, p. 31.
[535] Huntington, p. 58.
[536] Ibid, p. 364.

America since its founding."[537] Schlesinger argues that "Nationalism remains, after two centuries, the most vital political emotion in the world-far more vital than social ideologies such as communism or fascism or even democracy."[538] It is a chief impediment to Totalitarianism. As a result, the Socialist Progressives hold that nationalism must be removed in order for them to achieve their preferred state of cosmopolitanism.[539] Herein, the line of demarcation is set. The battle line is drawn.

"So it is that good warriors take their stand on ground where they cannot lose, and do not overlook conditions that make an opponent prone to defeat."[540]

The ground to defeat Progressive Socialist *ideology* which is anchored *in* Duocratic Totalitarianism is *the high ground.*

This is the ground upon which *The Founders* built America. It is the foundation upon which First Principles were established. This is the position to which Machiavelli encourages nations to "draw it back often toward its beginning" before their "goodness has been corrupted" and they have become "disordered."[541] Now is the time for America to *Return to First Principles*.

---

[537] Ibid, p. 365.
[538] Schlesinger, p. 53.
[539] Marx, pp. xiv-xvii.
[540] Sun Tzu, p. 29.
[541] Machiavelli, p. 209.

EPILOGUE

The history of liberty is the history of resistance ... [it is a]
history of the limitation of governmental power.
                          Woodrow Wilson (1856-1924)

Amerca is not well positioned to be a world leader in the 21ˢᵗ century. The country is socially decadent and economically it is on the brink of financial disaster. Much of America's government is self-serving. These are not the hallmarks that define a healthy and vibrant nation.

Since the early 1960s, socially, the United States has been on a Progressive road leading to destruction. As a result of this Socialist movement the United States is now the: 1) fifth highest nation in the world in failed marriages, 2) nation with the highest rate of teen pregnancy in the Western hemisphere and 3) country with the highest prison population in the world.

Since the early 1980s, economically, the United States has embraced a Libertarian, *laissez-faire* form of unbridled Capitalism. This paradigm has left the commercial and banking landscape of America in financial ruins. The Progressive-Libertarian experiment has caused the United States to find itself in the worst economic and financial shape since the Great Depression of the 1930s. Since the first edition of this book was published in 2009, there has been little improvement in the nation's banking system.

On October 31, 2011, the investment firm MF Global, had incurred a financial shortfall which had "ballooned to more than $1 billion."[542] It seems that "the firm had burned through a buffer of its own money and

---

[542] *The New York Times*. <u>MF Global's Shortfall No Surprise, Some Say</u>. Wednesday, March 28, 2012.

was using the cash of customers who were trading overseas" to meet the shortfall.[543]

On Tuesday, May 15, 2012 at a stockholder's meeting in Tampa, Florida, "the CEO of J. P. Morgan Chase offered a quick, but blunt apology to shareholders for a $2 billion trading loss that 'should never have happened'."[544] "The loss, disclosed Thursday, rattled investor confidence in the largest bank in the United States and the ability of Wall Street to meet regulatory changes more than three years after the financial crisis."[545] As this reckless behavior continues on Wall Street, the world teeters on the edge of financial ruin.

The Progressive-Socialists/Libertarians (Duoists) harbor a perverse Freudian characteristic which necessitates their having excessive control over other people's lives. Their thirst for power is never quenched and their appetite for monetary gain is never satisfied. They enact punitive tax legislation on the American people for personal gain. This is oftentimes accomplished through the distribution of tax dollars to so-called charitable organizations in which they have a vested interest. They are a corrupt group. Their nearly fifty years of work has evolved to the point of forging a *Totalitarian Duocracy* which must be derailed.

The Progressive-Socialists/Libertarians (Duoists) govern by: 1) continually increasing taxes on the American public, 2) confiscation of people's private property including their guns and 3) enacting unworkable and expensive programs that have harmful and lasting impacts on people's lives. They turn people's lives upside down, keeping them in a state of turmoil. There is never peace and harmony in the Progressive-Libertarian environment-only chaos and whirl.

If the Progressive-Socialist/Libertarian Movement (Duoism) is left to advance its newly contrived Communist-Nazi/*Laissez-faire* agenda, this is what will happen to America. The middle class will be financially drained. They will be ordered to fund an ever burdening Socialist *Nanny State* on one end, and be available to bailout giant corporations (General Motors) and banks (on the Too Big to Fail Theory) when they take huge losses from gambling in the marketplace on the other. This action drains the center financially. There will no longer be a middle-class in America. The Republic will be destroyed.

There will be an ever increasing number of American families living

---

543 Ibid.
544 www.Huffingtonpost.com
545 Ibid.

on the margin. Families will continue to disintegrate at an alarming rate ending in costly divorce lawsuits. An ever increasing number of children will fall behind and do poorly in school. The financial base for most Americans will continue to erode rapidly. If this trend is not reversed soon, more and more Americans will be falling toward the edge of poverty at an alarming rate. The United States will indeed be headed for disaster.

There will be a substantial increase in crime. Law enforcement officials will be unable to protect the masses. The reason being, their ability to care for the public will have been substantially limited due to restrictive laws enacted by the Progressive-Socialists/Libertarians, i.e., the Duocratic oligarchy now running the country.

The populace will have no way to protect themselves. The reason being, the Duocrats will have confiscated all of the citizenry's tools which ensures society's members individual safety and self preservation. The American people will be without money. They will live in unsafe environments controlled by criminal gangs. The majority of Americans will be rendered helpless, robbed of their liberty and living their daily lives in fear under totalitarian governance.

In going forward, the Free World economies must be Re-set.

The United States is hundreds of trillions of dollars in debt. Northern European banks hold fragile Southern European nation's debt on their balance sheets. Much of that debt is near worthless. In the meantime, Wall Street banks continue to engage in highly-leveraged, speculative trading of worthless swap and derivative paper. Federal government regulation is ineffective. In order for the United States to *Return to First Principles*, it must engage in a world-wide effort to re-set the economies of: 1) the European Union, 2) all of Latin America, 3) Central America, 4) Mexico, 5) Canada and 6) itself. To stabilize United States debt held by foreign nations, that debt must be monetized with Gold.

The American people must abandon their political party affiliations and join forces as Independents. They must mobilize and rise-up against an emerging tyranny. The goal is straightforward. Remove the Progressive-Socialist and Libertarian agendas from the American socioeconomic and political landscape and return the nation to First Principles. There is no other alternative if the United States is to remain a Republic and survive. There is no other recourse if the United States is to continue as a world leader in the 21st century.

Appendices

Appendix A – The Preamble to the Constitution of the United States.

Appendix B – Washington's Farewell Address 1796.

Appendix C – Thomas Jefferson First Inaugural Address.

Appendix D– The American's Creed.

Appendix E – The National Anthem of the United States of America (Stanza one).

Appendix F - The Pledge of Allegiance to the Flag

Appendix G – Health Care in America

Appendix H - The Socioeconomic and Political *Isms* Matrix

Appendix I – Public Service and Civil Liberties Organization Listing.

Appendix J – Small Group Activities and Topics for Discussion

Appendix K – Bank of America: Insider Trading

Appendix L – Citigroup Inc: Insider Trading

Appendix M – General Electric: Insider Trading

APPENDIX A

The PREAMBLE to the CONSTITUTION of the United States

We the People of the United States, in Order to form a more perfect Union, establish Justice, insure domestic Tranquility, provide for the common defense, promote the general Welfare, and secure the Blessings of Liberty to ourselves and our Posterity, do ordain and establish this Constitution for the United States of America.

APPENDIX B

WASHINGTON'S FAREWELL ADDRESS 1796

Friends and Citizens:

The period for a new election of a citizen to administer the executive government of the United States being not far distant, and the time actually arrived when your thoughts must be employed in designating the person who is to be clothed with that important trust, it appears to me proper, especially as it may conduce to a more distant expression of the public voice, that I should now apprise you of the resolution I have formed, to decline being considered among the number of those out of whom a choice is to be made.

I beg you, at the same time, to do me the justice to be assured that this resolution has not been taken without a strict regard to all the considerations appertaining to the relation which binds a dutiful citizen to his country; and that in withdrawing the tender of service, which silence in my situation might imply, I am influenced by no diminution of zeal for your future interest, no deficiency of grateful respect for your past kindness, but am supported by a full conviction that the step is compatible with both.

The acceptance of, and continuance hitherto in, the office to which your suffrages have twice called me have been a uniform sacrifice of inclination to the opinion of duty and to a deference for what appeared to be your desire. I constantly hoped that it would have been much earlier in my power, consistently with motives which I was not at liberty to disregard, to return to that retirement from which I had been reluctantly drawn. The strength of my inclination to do this, previous to the last election, had even led to the preparation of an address to declare it to you;

but mature reflection on the then perplexed and critical posture of our affairs with foreign nations, and the unanimous advice of persons entitled to my confidence, impelled me to abandon the idea.

I rejoice that the state of your concerns, external as well as internal, no longer renders the pursuit of inclination incompatible with the sentiment of duty or propriety, and am persuaded, whatever partiality may be retained for my services, that, in the present circumstances of our country, you will not disapprove my determination to retire.

The impressions with which I first undertook the arduous trust were explained on the proper occasion. In the discharge of this trust, I will only say that I have, with good intentions, contributed towards the organization and administration of the government the best exertions of which a very fallible judgment was capable. Not unconscious in the outset of the inferiority of my qualifications, experience in my own eyes, perhaps still more in the eyes of others, has strengthened the motives to diffidence of myself; and every day the increasing weight of years admonishes me more and more that the shade of retirement is as necessary to me as it will be welcome. Satisfied that if any circumstances have given peculiar value to my services, they were temporary. I have the consolation to believe that, while choice and prudence invite me to quit the political scene, patriotism does not forbid it.

In looking forward to the moment which is intended to terminate the career of my public life, my feelings do not permit me to suspend the deep acknowledgment of that debt of gratitude which I owe to my beloved country for the many honors it has conferred upon me; still more for the steadfast confidence with which it has supported me; and for the opportunities I have thence enjoyed of manifesting my inviolable attachment, by services faithful and preserving, though in usefulness unequal to my zeal. If benefits have resulted to our country from these services, let it always be remembered to your praise, and as an instructive example in our annals, that under circumstances in which the passions, agitated in every direction, were liable to mislead, amidst appearances sometimes dubious, vicissitudes of fortune often discouraging, in situations in which not unfrequently want of success has countenanced the spirit of criticism, the constancy of your support was the essential prop of the efforts, and a guarantee of the plans by which they were effected. Profoundly penetrated with this idea, I shall carry it with me to my grave, as a strong incitement to unceasing vows that heaven may continue to you the choicest tokens of its beneficence; that your union and brotherly affection may be perpetual; that the free Constitution, which is the work of your hands, may be sacredly maintained; that its administration in every department may be stamped with wisdom and virtue; that, in fine, the happiness of the people of these States, under the auspices of liberty, may be made complete by so careful a preservation and so prudent a use of this blessing as will acquire them the glory of recommending it to the applause, the affection, and adoption of every nation which is yet a stranger to it.

Here, perhaps, I ought to stop. But a solitude for your welfare, which cannot end but with my life, and the apprehension of danger, natural to that solicitude, urge me, on an occasion like the present, to offer to your solemn contemplation, and to recommend to your frequent review, some sentiments which are the result of much reflection, of no inconsiderable observation, and which appear to me all-important to the permanency of your felicity as a people. These will be offered to you with more freedom, as you can only see in them the disinterested warnings of a parting friend, who can possibly have no personal motive to bias his counsel. Nor can I forget, as an encouragement to it, your indulgent reception of my sentiments on a former and not dissimilar occasion.

Interwoven as is the love of liberty with every ligament of your hearts, no recommendation of mine is necessary to fortify or confirm the attachment. The unity of government which constitutes you one people is also now dear to you. It is justly so, for it is a main pillar in the edifice of your real independence, the support of your tranquility at home, your peace abroad; of your safety; of your prosperity; of that very liberty which you so highly prize. But as it is easy to foresee that, from different causes and from different quarters, much pains will be taken, many artifices employed to weaken in your minds the conviction of this truth; as this is the point in your political fortress against which the batteries of internal and external enemies will be most constantly and actively (though often covertly and insidiously) directed, it is of infinite moment that you should properly estimate the immense value of your national union to your collective and individual happiness; that you should cherish a cordial, habitual, and immovable attachment to it; accustoming yourselves to think and speak of it as of the palladium of your political safety and prosperity; watching for its preservation with jealous anxiety; discountenancing whatever may suggest even a suspicion that it can in any event be abandoned; and indignantly frowning upon the first dawning of every attempt to alienate any portion of our country from the rest, or to enfeeble the sacred ties which now link together the various parts.

For this you have every inducement of sympathy and interest. Citizens, by birth or choice, of a common country, that country has a right to concentrate your affections. The name American, which belongs to you in your national capacity, must always exalt the just pride of patriotism more than any appellation derived from local discriminations. With slight shades of difference, you have the same religion, manners, habits, and political principles. You have in a common cause fought and triumphed together; the independence and liberty you possess are the work of joint counsels, and joint efforts of common dangers, sufferings, and successes.

But these considerations, however powerfully they address themselves to your sensibility, are greatly outweighed by those which apply more immediately to your interest. Here every portion of our country finds the most commanding motives for carefully guarding and preserving the union of the whole.

The North, in an unrestrained intercourse with the South, protected by the equal laws of a common government, finds in the production of the latter great additional resources of maritime and commercial enterprise and precious materials of manufacturing industry. The South, in the same intercourse, benefiting by the agency of the North, sees its agriculture grow and its commerce expand. Turning partly into its own channels the seamen of the North, it finds its particular navigation invigorated; and, while it contributes, in different ways, to nourish and increase the general mass of the national navigation, it looks forward to the protection of a maritime strength, to which itself is unequally adapted. The East, in a like intercourse with the West, already finds, and in the progressive improvement of interior communications by land and water, will more and more find a valuable vent for the commodities which it brings from abroad, or manufacturing at home. The West derives from the East supplies requisite to its growth and comfort, and, what is perhaps of still greater consequence; it must of necessity owe the secure enjoyment of indispensable outlets for its own production to the weight, influence, and the future maritime strength of the Atlantic side of the Union, directed by an indissoluble community of interest as one nation. Any other tenure by which the West can hold this essential advantage, whether derived from its own separate strength, or from an apostate and unnatural connection with any foreign power, must be intrinsically precarious.

While, then, every part of our country thus feels an immediate and particular interest in union, all the parts combined cannot fail to find in the united mass of means and efforts greater strength, greater resource, proportionably greater security from external danger, a less frequent interruption of their peace by foreign nations; and, what is of inestimable value, they must derive from union an exemption from those broils and wars between themselves, which so frequently afflict neighboring countries not tied together by the same governments, which their own rival ships alone would be sufficient to produce, but which opposite foreign alliances, attachments, and intrigues would stimulate and embitter. Hence, likewise, they will avoid the necessity of those overgrown military establishments which, under any form of government, are inauspicious to liberty, and which are to be regarded as particularly hostile to republican liberty. In this sense it is that your union ought to be considered as a main prop of your liberty, and that the love of the one ought to endear to you the preservation of the other.

These considerations speak a persuasive language to every reflecting and virtuous mind, and exhibit the continuance of the Union as a primary object of patriotic desire. Is there a doubt whether a common government can embrace so large a sphere? Let experience solve it. To listen to mere speculation in such a case were criminal. We are authorized to hope that a proper organization of the whole with the auxiliary agency of governments for the respective subdivisions, will afford a happy issue to the experiment. It is well worth a fair and full experiment. With such powerful and obvious motives to union, affecting all parts of our country, while experience shall not have demonstrated its impracticability, there will always be reason to distrust the patriotism of those who in any quarter may endeavor to weaken its bands.

In contemplating the causes which may disturb our Union, it occurs as matter of serious concern that any ground should have been furnished for characterizing parties by geographical discrimination, Northern and

Southern, Atlantic and Western; whence designing men may endeavor to excite a belief that there is a real difference of local interests and views. One of the expedients of party to acquire influence within particular districts is to misrepresent the opinions and aims of other districts. You cannot shield yourselves too much against the jealousies and heartburnings which spring from these misrepresentations; they tend to render alien to each other those who ought to be bound together by fraternal affection. The inhabitants of our Western country have lately had a useful lesson on this head; they have seen, in the negotiation by the Executive, and in the unanimous ratification by the Senate, of the treaty with Spain, and in the universal satisfaction at the event, throughout the United States, a decisive proof how unfounded were the suspicions propagated among them of a policy in the General Government and in the Atlantic States unfriendly to their interests in regard to the Mississippi; they have been witnesses to the formation of two treaties, that with Great Britain, and that with Spain, which secure to them everything they could desire, in respect to our foreign relations, towards confirming their prosperity. Will it not be their wisdom to reply for the preservation of these advantages on the Union by which they were procured? Will they not henceforth be deaf to those advisers, if such there are, who would sever them from their brethren and connect them with aliens?

To the efficacy and permanency of your Union, a government for the whole is indispensable. No alliance, however strict, between the parts can be an adequate substitute; they must inevitably experience the infractions and interruptions which all alliances in all times have experienced. Sensible of this momentous truth, you have improved upon your first essay, by the adoption of a constitution of government better calculated than your former for an intimate union, and for the efficacious management of your common concerns. This government, the offspring of our own choice, uninfluenced and unawed, adopted upon full investigation and mature deliberation, completely free in its principles, in the distribution of its powers, uniting security with energy, and containing within itself a provision for its own amendment, has a just claim to your confidence and your support. Respect for its authority, compliance with its laws, acquiescence in its measures, are duties enjoined by the fundamental maxims of true liberty. The basis of our political systems is the right of the people to make and to alter their constitutions of government. But the **Constitution** which at any time exists, till changed by an explicit and authentic act of the whole people, is sacredly obligatory upon all. The very idea of the power and the right of the people to establish government presupposes the duty of every individual to obey the established government.

All obstructions to the execution of the laws, all combinations and associations, under whatever plausible character, with the real design to direct, control, counteract, or awe the regular deliberation and action of the constituted authorities, are destructive of this fundamental principle, and of fatal tendency. They serve to organize faction, to give it an artificial and extraordinary force; to put, in the place of the delegated will of the nation the will of a party, often a small but artful and enterprising minority of the community; and, according to the alternate triumphs of different parties, to make the public administration the mirror of the ill-concerted and incongruous projects of faction, rather than the organ of consistent and wholesome plans digested by common counsels and modified by mutual interests.

However combinations or associations of the above descriptions may now and then answer popular ends, they are likely, in the course of time and things, to become potent engines, by which cunning, ambitious, and unprincipled men will be enabled to subvert the power of the people and to usurp for themselves the reins of government, destroying afterwards the very engines which have lifted them to unjust dominion.

Towards the preservation of your government, and the permanency of your present happy state, it is requisite, not only that you steadily discountenance irregular oppositions to its acknowledged authority, but also that you resist with care the spirit of innovation upon its principles, however specious the pretexts. One method of assault may be to effect, in the forms of the **Constitution**, alterations which will impair the energy of the system, and thus to undermine what cannot be directly overthrown. In all the changes to which you may be invited, remember that time and habit are at least as necessary to fix the true character of government as of other human institutions; that experience is the surest standard by which to test the real tendency of the existing constitution of a country; that facility in changes, upon the credit of mere hypothesis and opinion, exposes to perpetual change, from the endless variety of hypothesis and opinion; and remember, especially, that for the efficient management of your common interests, in a country so extensive as ours, a government of as much vigor as is consistent with the perfect security of liberty is indispensable. Liberty itself will find in such a government, with powers properly distributed and adjusted, its surest guardian. It is, indeed, little else than a name, where the government is too feeble to withstand the enterprises of faction, to confine each member of the society within the limits prescribed by the laws, and to maintain all in the secure and tranquil enjoyment of the rights of person and property.

I have already intimated to you the danger of parties in the State, with particular reference to the founding of them on geographical discriminations. Let me now take a more comprehensive view, and warn you in the most solemn manner against the baneful effects of the spirit of party generally.

This spirit, unfortunately, is inseparable from our nature, having its root in the strongest passions of the human mind. It exists under different shapes in all governments, more or less stifled, controlled, or repressed; but, in those of the popular form, it is seen in its greatest rankness, and is truly their worst enemy.

The alternate domination of one faction over another, sharpened by the spirit of revenge, natural to party dissension, which in different ages and countries has perpetrated the most horrid enormities, is itself a frightful despotism. But this leads at length to a more formal and permanent despotism. The disorders and miseries which result gradually incline the minds of men to seek security and repose in the absolute power of an individual; and sooner or later the chief of some prevailing faction, more able or more fortunate than his competitors, turns this disposition to the purposes of his own elevation, on the ruins of public liberty.

Without looking forward to an extremity of this kind (which nevertheless ought not to be entirely out of sight), the common and continual mischiefs of the spirit of party are sufficient to make it the interest and duty of a wise people to discourage and restrain it.

It serves always to distract the public councils and enfeeble the public administration. It agitates the community with ill-founded jealousies and false alarms, kindles the animosity of one part against another, foments occasionally riot and insurrection. It opens the door to foreign influence and corruption, which finds a facilitated access to the government itself through the channels of party passions. Thus the policy and the will of one country are subjected to the policy and will of another.

There is an opinion that parties in free countries are useful checks upon the administration of the government and serve to keep alive the spirit of liberty. This within certain limits is probably true; and in governments of a monarchical cast, patriotism may look with indulgence, if not with favor, upon the spirit of party. But in those of the popular character, in governments purely elective, it is a spirit not to be encouraged. From their natural tendency, it is certain there will always be enough of that spirit for every salutary purpose. And there being constant danger of excess, the effort ought to be by force of public opinion, to mitigate and assuage it. A fire not to be quenched, it demands a uniform vigilance to prevent its bursting into a flame, lest, instead of warming, it should consume.

It is important, likewise, that the habits of thinking in a free country should inspire caution in those entrusted with its administration, to confine themselves within their respective constitutional spheres, avoiding in the exercise of the powers of one department to encroach upon another. The spirit of encroachment tends to consolidate the powers of all the departments in one, and thus to create, whatever the form of government, a real despotism. A just estimate of that love of power, and proneness to abuse it, which predominates in the human heart, is sufficient to satisfy us of the truth of this position. The necessity of reciprocal checks in the exercise of political power, by dividing and distributing it into different depositaries, and constituting each the guardian of the public weal against invasions by the others, has been evinced by experiments ancient and modern; some of them in our country and under our own eyes. To preserve them must be as necessary as to institute them. If, in the opinion of the people, the distribution or modification of the constitutional powers be in any particular wrong, let it be corrected by an amendment in the way which the **Constitution** designates. But let there be no change by usurpation; for though this, in one instance, may be the instrument of good, it is the customary weapon by which free governments are destroyed. The precedent must always greatly overbalance in permanent evil any partial or transient benefit, which the use can at any time yield.

Of all the dispositions and habits which lead to political prosperity, religion and morality are indispensable supports. In vain would that man claim the tribute of patriotism, who should labor to subvert these great pillars of human happiness, these firmest props of the duties of men and citizens. The mere politician, equally with the pious man, ought to respect and to cherish them. A volume could not trace all their connections with private and public felicity. Let it simply be asked: Where is the security for property, for reputation, for life, if the sense of religious obligation desert the oaths which are the instruments of investigation in courts of justice? And let us with caution indulge the supposition that morality can be maintained without religion. Whatever may be conceded to the influence of refined education on minds of peculiar structure, reason and experience both forbid us to expect that national morality can prevail in exclusion of religious principle.

It is substantially true that virtue or morality is a necessary spring of popular government. The rule, indeed, extends with more or less force to every species of free government. Who that is a sincere friend to it can look with indifference upon attempts to shake the foundation of the fabric?

Promote then, as an object of primary importance, institutions for the general diffusion of knowledge. In proportion as the structure of a government gives force to public opinion, it is essential that public opinion should be enlightened.

As a very important source of strength and security, cherish public credit. One method of preserving it is to use it as sparingly as possible, avoiding occasions of expense by cultivating peace, but remembering also that timely disbursements to prepare for danger frequently prevent much greater disbursements to repel it, avoiding likewise the accumulation of debt, not only by shunning occasions of expense, but by vigorous exertion in time of peace to discharge the debts which unavoidable wars may have occasioned, not ungenerously throwing upon posterity the burden which we ourselves ought to bear. The execution of these maxims belongs to your representatives, but it is necessary that public opinion should cooperate. To facilitate to them the performance of their duty, it is essential that you should practically bear in mind that towards the payment of debts there must be revenue; that to have revenue there must be taxes; that no taxes can be devised which are not more or less inconvenient and unpleasant; that the intrinsic embarrassment, inseparable from the selection of the proper objects (which is always a choice of difficulties), ought to be a decisive motive for a candid construction of the conduct of the government in making it, and for a spirit of acquiescence in the measures for obtaining revenue, which the public exigencies may at any time dictate.

Observe good faith and justice towards all nations; cultivate peace and harmony with all. Religion and morality enjoin this conduct; and can it be, that good policy does not equally enjoin it? It will be worthy of a free, enlightened, and at no distant period, a great nation, to give to mankind the magnanimous and too novel example of a people always guided by an exalted justice and benevolence. Who can doubt that, in the course of time and things, the fruits of such a plan would richly repay any temporary advantages which might be lost by a steady adherence to it? Can it be that Providence has not connected the permanent felicity of a nation with its virtue? The experiment, at least, is recommended by every sentiment which ennobles human nature. Alas! Is it rendered impossible by its vices?

In the execution of such a plan, nothing is more essential than that permanent, inveterate antipathies against particular nations, and passionate attachments for others, should be excluded; and that, in place of them, just and amicable feelings towards all should be cultivated. The nation which indulges towards another a habitual hatred or a habitual fondness is in some degree a slave. It is a slave to its animosity or to its affection, either of which is sufficient to lead it astray from its duty and its interest. Antipathy in one nation against another disposes each more readily to offer insult and injury, to lay hold of slight causes of umbrage, and to be haughty and intractable, when accidental or trifling occasions of dispute occur. Hence, frequent collisions, obstinate, envenomed, and bloody contests. The nation, prompted by ill-will and resentment, sometimes impels to war the government, contrary to the best calculations of policy. The government sometimes participates in the national propensity, and adopts through passion what reason would reject; at other times it makes the animosity of the nation subservient to projects of hostility instigated by pride, ambition, and other sinister and pernicious motives. The peace of ten, sometimes perhaps the liberty, of nations, has been the victim.

So likewise, a passionate attachment of one nation for another produces a variety of evils. Sympathy for the favorite nation, facilitating the illusion of an imaginary common interest in cases where no real common interest exists, and infusing into one the enmities of the other, betrays the former into a participation in the quarrels and wars of the latter without adequate inducement or justification. It leads also to concessions to the favorite nation of privileges denied to others which is aptly doubly to injure the nation making the concessions; by unnecessarily parting with what ought to have been retained, and by exciting jealousy, ill-will, and a disposition to retaliate, in the parties from whom equal privileges are withheld. And it gives to ambitious, corrupted, or deluded citizens (who devote themselves to the favorite nation), facility to betray or sacrifice the interests of their own country, without odium, sometimes even with popularity; gilding, with the appearance of a virtuous sense of obligation, a commendable deference for public opinion, or a laudable zeal for public good, the base or foolish compliance of ambition, corruption, or infatuation.

As avenues to foreign influence in innumerable ways, such attachments are particularly alarming to the truly enlightened and independent patriot. How many opportunities do they afford to tamper with domestic factions, to practice the arts of seduction, to mislead public opinion, to influence or awe the public councils? Such an attachment of a small or weak towards a great and powerful nation dooms the former to be the satellite of the latter.

Against the insidious wiles of foreign influence (I conjure you to believe me, fellow-citizens) the jealousy of a free people ought o be constantly awake, since history and experience prove that foreign influence is one of the most baneful foes of republican government. But that jealousy to be useful must be impartial; else it becomes the instrument of the very influence to be avoided, instead of a defense against it. Excessive partiality for one foreign nation and excessive dislike of another cause those whom they actuate to see danger only on one side, and serve to veil and even second that arts of influence on the other. Real patriots who may resist the intrigues of the favorite are liable to become suspected and odious, while its tools and dupes usurp the applause and confidence of the people, to surrender their interests.

The great rule of conduct for us in regard to foreign nations is in extending our commercial relations, to have with them as little political connection as possible. So far as we have already formed engagements, let them be fulfilled with perfect good faith. Here let us stop. Europe has a set of primary interests which to us have none; or a very remote relation. Hence she must be engaged in frequent controversies, the causes of which are essentially foreign to our concerns. Hence, therefore, it must be unwise in us to implicate ourselves by artificial ties in the ordinary vicissitudes of her politics, or the ordinary combinations and collisions of her friendships or enmities.

Our detached and distant situation invites and enables us to pursue a different course. If we remain one people under an efficient government, the period is not far off when we may defy material injury from external annoyance; when we may take such an attitude as will cause the neutrality we may at any time resolve upon to be scrupulously respected; when belligerent nations, under the impossibility of making acquisitions upon us, will not lightly hazard the giving us provocation; when we may choose peace or war, as our interests, guided by justice, shall counsel.

Why forego the advantages of so peculiar a situation? Why quit our own to stand upon foreign ground? Why, by interweaving our destiny with that of any part of Europe, entangle our peace and prosperity in the toils of European ambition, rivalship, interest, humor or caprice?

It is our true policy to steer clear of permanent alliances with any portion of the foreign world; so far, I mean, as we are now at liberty to do it; for let me not be understood as capable of patronizing infidelity to existing engagements. I hold the maxim no less applicable to public than to private affairs, that honesty is always the best policy. I repeat it, therefore, let those engagements be observed in their genuine sense. But, in my opinion, it is unnecessary and would be unwise to extend them.

Taking care always to keep ourselves by suitable establishments on a respectable defensive posture, we may safely trust to temporary alliances for extraordinary emergencies.

Harmony, liberal intercourse with all nations, are recommended by policy, humanity, and interest. But even our commercial policy should hold an equal and impartial hand; neither seeking nor granting exclusive favors or preferences; consulting the natural course of things; diffusing and diversifying by gentle means the streams of commerce, but forcing nothing; establishing (with powers so disposed, in order to give trade a stable course, to define the rights of our merchants, and to enable the government to support them) conventional rules of intercourse, the best that present circumstances and mutual opinion will permit, but temporary, and liable to be from time to time abandoned or varied, as experience and circumstances shall dictate; constantly keeping in view that it is folly in one nation to look for disinterested favors from another; that it must pay with a portion of its independence for whatever it may accept under that character; that, by such acceptance, it may place itself in the condition of having given equivalents for nominal favors, and yet of being reproached with ingratitude for not giving more. There can be no greater error than to expect or calculate upon real favors from nation to nation. It is an illusion, which experience must cure, which a just pride ought to discard.

In offering to you, my countrymen, these counsels of an old and affectionate friend, I dare not hope they will make the strong and lasting impression I could wish; that they will control the usual current of the passions, or prevent our nation from running the course which has hitherto marked the destiny of nations. But, if I may even flatter myself that they may be productive of some partial benefit, some occasional good; that they may now and then recur to moderate the fury of party spirit, to warn against the mischiefs of foreign intrigue, to guard against the impostures of pretended patriotism; this hope will be a full recompense for the solicitude for your welfare, by which they have been dictated.

How far in the discharge of my official duties I have been guided by the principles which have been delineated, the public records and other evidences of my conduct must witness to you and to the world. To myself, the assurance of my own conscience is, that I have at least believed myself to be guided by them.

In relation to the still subsisting war in Europe, my proclamation of the twenty-second of April, 1793, is the index of my plan. Sanctioned by your approving voice, and by that of your representatives in both houses of Congress, the spirit of that measure has continually governed me, uninfluenced by any attempts to deter or divert me from it.

After deliberate examination, with the aid of the best lights I could obtain, I was well satisfied that our country, under all the circumstances of the case, had a right to take, and was bound in duty and interest to take, a neutral position. Having taken it, I determined, as far as should depend upon me, to maintain it, with moderation, perseverance, and firmness.

The considerations which respect the right to hold this conduct, it is not necessary on this occasion to detail. I will only observe that, according to my understanding of the matter, that right, so far from being denied by any of the belligerent powers, has been virtually admitted by all.

The duty of holding a neutral conduct may be inferred, without anything more, from the obligation which justice and humanity impose on every nation, in cases in which it is free to act, to maintain inviolate the relations of peace and amity towards other nations.

The inducements of interest for observing that conduct will best be referred to your own reflections and experience. With me a predominant motive has been to endeavor to gain time to our country to settle and mature its yet recent institutions, and to progress without interruption to that degree of strength and consistency which is necessary to give it, humanly speaking, the command of its own fortunes.

Though, in reviewing the incidents of my administration, I am unconscious of intentional error, I am nevertheless too sensible of my defects not to think it probably that I may have committed many errors. Whatever they may be, I fervently beseech the Almighty to avert or mitigate the evils to which they may tend. I shall also carry with me the hope that my country will never cease to view them with indulgence; and that, after forty five years of my life dedicated to its service with an upright zeal, the faults of incompetent abilities will be consigned to oblivion, as myself must soon be to the mansions of rest.

Relying on its kindness in this as in other things, and actuated by that fervent love towards it, which is so natural to a man who views in it the native soil of himself and his progenitors for several generations, I anticipate with pleasing expectation that retreat in which I promise myself to realize, without alloy, the sweet enjoyment of partaking, in the midst of my fellow-citizens, the benign influence of good laws under a free government, the ever-favorite object of my heart, and the happy reward, as I trust, of our mutual cares, labors and dangers.

Geo. Washington

SOURCE:
Copyright 1996 The Avalon Project at Yale Law School.
The Avalon Project: Washington's Farewell Address 1796
last modified on: 02/02/2008.

APPENDIX C

THOMAS JEFFERSON FIRST INAUGURAL ADDRESS

First Inaugural Address
March 4, 1801

Friends and Fellow-Citizens

Called upon to undertake the duties of the first executive office of our country, I avail myself of the presence of that portion of my fellow-citizens which is here assembled to express my grateful thanks for the favor with which they have been pleased to look toward me, to declare a sincere consciousness that the task is above my talents, and that I approach it with those anxious and awful presentiments which the greatness of the charge and the weakness of my powers so justly inspire. A rising nation, spread over a wide and fruitful land, traversing all the seas with the rich productions of their industry, engaged in commerce with nations who feel power and forget right, advancing rapidly to destinies beyond the reach of mortal eye –when I contemplate these transcendent objects, and see the honor, the happiness, and the hopes of this beloved country committed to the issue and the auspices of this day, I shrink from the contemplation, and humble myself before the magnitude of the undertaking. Utterly, indeed, should I despair did not the presence of many whom I here see remind me that in the other high authorities provided by our **Constitution** I shall find resources of wisdom, of virtue, and of zeal on which to rely under all difficulties. To you, then, gentlemen, who are charged with the sovereign functions of legislation, and to those associated with you, I look with encouragement for that guidance and support which may enable us to steer with safety the vessel in which we are all embarked amidst the conflicting elements of a troubled world.

During the contest of opinion through which we have passed the animation of discussions and of exertions has sometimes worn an aspect which might impose on strangers unused to think freely and to speak and to write what they think; but this being now decided by the voice of the nation, announced according to the rules of the **Constitution,** all will, of course, arrange themselves under the will of the law, and unite in common efforts for the common good. All, too, will bear in mind this sacred principle, that though the will of the majority is in all cases to prevail, that will to be rightful must be reasonable; that the minority possess their equal rights, which equal law must protect, and to violate would be oppression. Let us, then, fellow-citizens, unite with one heart and one mind. Let us restore to social intercourse that harmony and affection without which liberty and even life itself are but dreary things. And let us reflect that having banished from our land that religious intolerance under which mankind so long bled and suffered, we have yet gained little if we countenance a political intolerance as despotic, as wicked, and capable of as bitter and bloody persecutions. During the throes and convulsions of the ancient world, during the agonizing spasms of infuriated man, seeking through blood and slaughter his long-lost liberty, it was not wonderful that the agitation of the billows should reach even this distant and peaceful shore; that this should be more felt and feared by some and less by others, and should divide opinions as to measures of safety. But every difference of opinion is not a difference of principle. We have called by different names brethren of the same principle. We are all Republicans, we are all Federalists. If there be any among us who would wish to dissolve this Union or to change its republican form, let them stand undisturbed as monuments of the safety with which error of opinion may be tolerated where reason is left free to combat it. I know, indeed, that some honest men fear that a republican government can not be strong, that this Government is not strong enough; but would the honest patriot, in the full tide of successful experiment, abandon a government which has so far kept us free and firm on the theoretic and visionary fear that this Government, the world's best hope, may by possibility want energy to preserve itself? I trust not. I believe this, on the contrary, the strongest Government on earth. I believe it the only one where every man, at the call of the law, would fly to the standard of the law, and would meet invasions of the public order as his own personal concern.

Sometimes it is said that man can not be trusted with the government of himself. Can he, then, be trusted with the government of others? Or have we found angels in the forms of kings to govern him? Let history answer this question.

Let us, then, with courage and confidence pursue our own Federal and Republican principles, our attachment to union and representative government. Kindly separated by nature and a wide ocean from the exterminating havoc of one quarter of the globe; too high-minded to endure the degradations of the others; possessing a chosen country, with room enough for our descendants to the thousandth and thousandth generation; entertaining a due sense of our equal right to the use of our own faculties, to the acquisitions of our own industry, to honor and confidence from our fellow-citizens, resulting not from birth, but from our actions and their sense of them; enlightened by a benign religion, professed, indeed, and practiced in various forms, yet all of them inculcating honesty, truth, temperance, gratitude, and the love of man; acknowledging and adoring an overruling Providence, which by all its dispensations proves that it delights in the happiness of man here and his greater happiness hereafter—with all these blessings, what more is necessary to make us a happy and a prosperous people? Still one thing more fellow-citizens—a wise and frugal Government, which shall restrain men from injuring one another, shall leave them otherwise free to regulate their own pursuits of industry and improvement, and shall not take from the mouth of labor the bread it has earned. This is the sum of good government, and this is necessary to close the circle of our felicities.

About to enter, felloe-citizens, on the exercise of duties which comprehend everything dear and valuable to you, it is proper you should understand what I deem the essential principles of our Government, and consequently those which ought to shape its Administration. I will compress them within the narrowest compass they will bear, stating the general principle, but not all its limitations. Equal and exact justice to all men, of whatever state or persuasion, religious or political; peace, commerce, and honest friendship with all nations, entangling alliances with none; the support of the State governments in all their rights, as the most competent administrations for our domestic concerns and the surest bulwarks against antirepublican tendencies; the preservation of the General Government in its whole constitutional vigor, as the sheet anchor of our peace at home and safety abroad; a jealous care of the right of election by the people-a mild and safe corrective of abuses which are lopped by the sword of revolution where peaceable remedies are unprovided; absolute acquiescence in the decisions of the majority, the vital principle of republics, from which is no appeal but to force, the vital principle and immediate parent of despotism; a well-disciplined militia, our best reliance in peace and for the first moments of war till regulars may relieve them; the supremacy of the civil over the military authority; economy in the public expense, that labor may be lightly burthened; the honest payment of our debts and sacred preservation of the public faith; encouragement of agriculture, and of commerce as its handmaid; the diffusion of information and arraignment of all abuses at the bar of the public reason; freedom of religion; freedom of the press, and freedom of person under the protection of the habeas corpus, and trial by juries impartially selected. These principles form the bright constellation which has gone before us and guided our steps through an age of revolution and reformation. The wisdom of our sages and blood of our heroes have been devoted to their attainment. They should be the creed of our political faith, the text of civic instruction, the touchstone by which to try the services of those we trust; and should we wander from them in moments of error or of alarm, let us hasten to retrace our steps and to regain the road which alone leads to peace, liberty, and safety.

I repair, then, fellow-citizens, to the post you have assigned me. With experience enough in subordinate offices to have seen the difficulties of this the greatest of all, I have learnt to expect that it will rarely fall to the lot of imperfect man to retire from this station with the reputation and the favor which bring him into it. Without pretensions to that high confidence you reposed in our first and greatest revolutionary character, whose preeminent services had entitled him to the first place in his country's love and destined for him fairest page in the volume of faithful history, I ask so much confidence only as may give firmness and effect to the legal administration of your affairs. I shall often go wrong through defect of judgment. When right, I shall often be thought wrong by those whose positions will not command a view of the whole ground. I ask your indulgence for my own errors, which will never be intentional, and your support against the errors of others, who may condemn what they would not if seen in all its parts. The approbation implied by your suffrage is a great consolation for me for the past, and my future solicitude will be to retain the good opinion of those who have bestowed it in advance, to conciliate that of others by doing them all the good in my power, and to be instrumental to the happiness and freedom of all.

Relying, then, on the patronage of your good will, I advance with obedience to the work, ready to retire from it whenever you become sensible how much better choice it is in your power to make. And may that Infinite Power which rules the destinies of the universe lead our councils to what is best, and give them a favorable issue for your peace and prosperity.

SOURCE:
Copyright 1996 The Avalon Project at Yale Law School
The Avalon Project: Jefferson's First Inaugural Address
last modified on: 02/01/2008

APPENDIX D

THE AMERICAN'S CREED
By: William Tyler Page

I believe in the United States of America as a Government of the People, by the People, for the People; whose just powers are derived from the consent of the governed; A democracy in a republic, a sovereign Nation of many Sovereign States; a perfect Union, one and inseparable; established upon those principles of Freedom, Equality, Justice, and Humanity for which American Patriots sacrificed their Lives and Fortunes.

I therefore believe it is my duty to my country to Love it; to Support its *Constitution*; to obey its laws; to Respect its Flag; and to defend it against all enemies.

APPENDIX E

The NATIONAL ANTHEM of
the United States of America

O! say can you see by the dawn's early light,
What so proudly we hailed at the twilight's last
gleaming,
Whose broad stripes and bright stars through the
perilous fight,
O'er the ramparts we watched, were so gallantly
streaming?
and the rockets' red glare, the bombs bursting in
air,
Gave proof through the night that our flag was still
there;
O! say does that star-spangled banner yet wave,
O'er the land of the free and the home of the
brave?
Stanza One.

APPENDIX F

THE PLEDGE OF ALLEGIANCE

I Pledge Allegiance to the flag of the United States of
America and to the *Republic* for which it stands,
One Nation under God,
indivisible, with liberty and justice for all.

APPENDIX G

HEALTH CARE IN AMERICA

The year 1811 was a painful and difficult year for John and Abigail Smith Adams. That year, their daughter, Abigail "Nabby" Adams "had discovered a 'hardness' in her right breast."[546]

> "She consulted with Cotton Tufts and several physicians in Boston and wrote to Benjamin Rush for his advice. The Boston doctors all advised the surgical removal of her breast, as did Rush in a thoughtful letter to her father. He preferred giving his opinion this way, Rush told Adams, so that he and Abigail could 'communicate it gradually.'
>
> From the experience of more than fifty years in such cases, Rush said, he knew but one remedy, 'the knife'. 'From her account of the *moving* state of the tumor, it is now in a proper situation for the operation. Should she wait till it superates or even inflames much, it may be too late…. I repeat again, let there be no delay…. Her time of life calls for expedition in this business, for tumors such as hers tend much more rapidly to cancer after 45 than in more early life.' Nabby was forty-six.
>
> A mastectomy was performed on Nabby in the bedroom beside that of her mother and father on October 8. As Adams wrote to Rush, the operation took twenty-five minutes, the dressing an hour longer. The agony she endured in that day before anesthetics is unimaginable.

---

[546] McCullough, p. 602.

The four surgeons who performed the operation told Adams afterward that they had never known a patient to show such fortitude."[547]

Abigail "Nabby" Adams died on August 15, 1813.

It is absolutely shameful that, in nearly 200 years, the United States has made no significant progress in finding a cure for breast cancer. America has little to show for the hundreds of millions of dollars spent over several decades trying to discover cures for the various forms of cancer. As to the victims of this terrible disease and their families, the war on cancer has been a dismal failure.

Gina Kolata is a columnist for the New York Times. In her article How Bright Promise in Cancer testing Fell Apart she reported that lung cancer patient, Juliet Jacobs, entered a research study at Duke University in February 2010. "Doctors would assess her tumor cells, looking for gene patterns that would determine which drugs would best attack her particular cancer."[548] "The Duke Program – was the first fruit of the new genomics, a way of letting a cancer cell's own genes reveal the cancer's weaknesses."[549] "But the research at Duke turned out to be wrong. Its gene based tests proved worthless, and the research behind them was discredited."[550] Ms. Jacobs died shortly after treatment.

Health Care in America is Wrongheaded.

Nabby Adams and Juliet Jacobs are just two examples of the tens of thousands of people who die of cancer every year. The chief reason this happens is because the focus of the health care system in the United States is on treating sick people and **not** seeking cures for the most pressing diseases. Critics have long maintained that America's health care program operates first, for the financial benefit of those in the insurance and medical profession. The saving of patient's lives is secondary. This medical paradigm is upside-down; it is unacceptable and must be changed now.

---

[547] Ibid.
[548] Kolata, Gina. How Bright Promise in Cancer Testing Fell Apart. The New York Times. Friday, July 8, 2011, p. 1.
[549] Ibid.
[550] Ibid.

**In a decadent industry plagued with corruption
and greed, emerges certain organizations
dedicated to seeking cures for cancer.**

Founded in 1976, the biotechnology corporation Genentech was formed with the idea of recasting treatment for a number of serious diseases including cancer. Founders of the company, Robert Swanson and Dr. Herbert W. Boyer, were desirous of creating a new application of therapy by "genetically engineering the molecules that are most important in general human health."[551] The company has made great strides in the treatment of breast cancer with its drug *Herception*, and must be commended for its advancements.

Founded in 1929, Jackson Laboratories is part of a joint-venture which includes the University of Connecticut and Yale University designed to become a world leader in human genomic medical research. The group hopes to gain a better understanding of the role genetics plays in the diagnosis and treatment of cancer. This partnership offers exciting possibilities and provides hope to those persons who will be diagnosed with this dreadful disease. Jackson Laboratories, the University of Connecticut and Yale University must too, be commended for their courage and dedication in seeking a meaningful cure for cancer.

**America's medical industry should take their queue from
Genentech, Jackson Laboratories, the University of Connecticut
and Yale University in redesigning the nation's medical profession.**

The American Medical Association must recast its Mission Statement. It should read: "The primary goal of medical care in America is first, to seek cures for deadly diseases and second, the treating of ill and injured patients." The nation's health care industry must be entirely redirected.

The organization and management of America's health system must be overhauled. At present, these functions are shared primarily between the federal government and the private sector. This arrangement leads to an amalgamation of incompetence (the federal government) and self-serving, conflicts of interest (the private sector). The administration and management of America's health care industry should be centralized at each state's public university medical schools. It is in these institutions

---

[551] Genentech Inc. Research and Development. www.gene.com

where research should be conducted. The focus must be on finding cures of deadly diseases such as cancer.

First, the care and operation of hospitals and medical care facilities would come under the care of medical colleges in each state. Second, Medicare would be transferred to the states for administration. Third, the function of the federal government would be limited to making supplemental health care payments to states that may be experiencing a funding shortfall in the administration of their health care program.

The staffing of hospitals and medical facilities for patient care needs to be re-designed. The role of registered nurses should be expanded. The education and functions of physician's assistants would be enhanced substantially to include most responsibilities now associated with general medical practitioners. The use of medical technology would be brought to the next level, and the use of high-end surgeons would be expanded. The center of today's bloated middle sector of health care would by design, collapse. In other words, the revised medical system would include nurses, physician's assistants and high-end technological geared surgeons. Funds that are currently directed to that costly *center* would be re-directed toward research for the seeking of cures of catastrophic illnesses.

Citizen's Responsibility.

It is each person's duty and obligation to be responsible for their health. This begins with education of the polity in schools beginning in the first grade and extending through the twelfth grade of high schools. The citizenry must have an understanding of what they can expect from America's medical profession. As a first step, Americans should be aware of foods that harm and foods that heal. Second, people must be made conscious of the harmful effects of obesity and how to deal with that condition effectively. Third, the dangerous consequences associated with the use of tobacco products and alcohol, especially by teens and young adults. It shortens lives and enhances the costs of medical care in the United States. Drug addiction often requires expensive medical treatment programs and frequently leads to serious criminal activities.

Healthy nations are productive nations. Countries, whose populations are healthy, frequently enjoy a high standard of living and good quality of life. In the proposed medical program, all states would incorporate a feature which would provide for each of their citizenry to have a complete physical examination at least every two years. Preventive medicine goes a long way in heading off catastrophic illnesses before it reaches terminal stages. Within the state's Medicare programs would be a provision for each person to have their teeth cleaned once a year. Oral hygiene is critical to overall good physical health. All Americans deserve nothing but the best when it comes to medical care for the nation's citizenry.

APPENDIX H

The Socioeconomic and Political *Isms* Matrix

<u>Socioeconomic and Political Theories – Far Left of Center</u>
Communism – Karl Marx
Nazism – Adolph Hitler
Fascism – Benito Mussolini
Totalitarianism – Giovanni Gentile

<u>Social Theory – Left of Center</u>
Post Modern Progressivism – Woodrow Wilson
Modern Progressivism – Theodore Roosevelt
Welfarism – Jeremy Bentham

<u>Economic Theory – Left of Center</u>
Welfarism – John Maynard Keynes

<u>Socioeconomic and Political Theory – Center</u>
Classic Liberalism – John Locke

<u>Social Theory – Right of Center</u>
Egoism – Ayn Rand

<u>Economic Theory – Right of Center</u>
Capitalistic Economic Theory – Adam Smith

<u>Economic Theory – Far Right of Center</u>
Libertarian Economic Theory – Milton Friedman

NOTE: Duoism is a newly discovered emerging socioeconomic and political *idea* in America. Its social model is *Marxist-Socialism*. The commercial and economic paradigm is *Libertarianism*. Because these two "isms" are diametrically opposed and completely incompatible, Duoism's political model is *Totalitarian*. It has to be. Duoism draws from *Nazism* to manage these conflicting "isms." It controls the masses through the implementation of required *Politically Correct* speech codes. Liberty for the body politic is lost. See the Glossary of Selected Terms.

APPENDIX I

═══

Public Service and Civil Liberties Organization Listing

American Center for Law and Justice (Conservative)
P.O. Box 90555
Washington, DC 20090-0555
(800) 296-4529

American Civil Liberties Union (Progressive)
125 Broad Street
18th Floor
New York, NY 10004
(212) 549-2500

Americans for Democratic Action (Progressive)
1625 K Street, NW
Suite 102
Washington, DC 20006
(202) 785-5980

Foundation for Individual Rights in Education (Neutral)
601 Walnut Street
Suite 510
Philadelphia, PA 19106
(215) 717-3473

Rutherford Institute, The (Conservative)
P.O. Box 7482
Charlottesville, VA 22906-7482
(434) 978-3888

Southern Poverty Law Center (Progressive)
400 Washington Avenue
Montgomery, AL 36104
(334) 956-8200

Thomas More Law Center (Conservative)
24 Frank Lloyd Wright Drive
P.O. Box 393
Ann Arbor, MI 48106(734) 827-2001

APPENDIX J

Small Group Activities and Topics for Discussion

- Participation by parent or PTA committees in the selection of school textbooks and curricula formulation.

- The development of Action Plans to have Tax Codes modified to benefit a stay at home parent arrangement, a commonality of the 21st century.

- Meetings between school officials and parents accompanied by carefully selected lawyers, for the purpose of dismantling "Political Correctness" from the classroom and replace that tyrannical linguistic format with "Responsible Speech." Engage *FIRE* in Philadelphia, and like minded organizations, for Action Plan assistance

- Organizing a campaign to have state representatives pass legislation that would overturn politically correct *Speech Codes*.

- Work with local and state bar associations to bring about meaningful tort reform and establishing procedures to remove corrupt judges from the bench.

- Small group conferences (with carefully selected local attorneys) that focus on ways to engage Marxist-Socialist activists in court actions.

- Discussions relating to the benefits, risks and procedures involved in calling for a Constitutional Convention.

- The examination and aggressive use of the impeachment process.

- Exploring ways to install a nationwide voting machinery capability that is uncomplicated and eliminates any possibility of ballot box fraud.

- The advisability of working toward the passing of Constitutional amendments to seek term limits for the President and members of Congress.

- Identification of methods and requirements for removing corrupt officials on the local, state and national levels.

- Determine community activities that will contribute to public safety.

- Conferences with key legislators in regard to reforming the criminal and juvenile justice systems.

APPENDIX K

BANK OF AMERICA CORP: INSIDER TRADING

02/06/09
Thomas M. Ryan
Purchased 25,000 shares @ $5.60

02/06/09
Brian T. Moynihan
Purchased 10,000 shares @ $4.80

02/06/09
Walter Massey
Purchased 2,000 shares @ $6.21

02/17/09
Jacquelyn Ward
Purchased 9,900 shares @ $5.05

02/20/09
Jacquelyn Ward
Purchased 13,100 shares @ $3.78

52 week low price: $2.53
Closing Price (05/12/09): $12.70

SOURCE:
Moneycentral.msn.com
Insider Trading Transactions and Stock Quote
Date: 05/12/09

APPENDIX L

CITIGROUP INC: INSIDER TRADING

03/03/09
Lewis B. Kaden
Purchased 100,000 shares @ $1.26

03/03/09
Manuel Medina
Purchased 1.5 million shares @ $1.24

03/03/09
John C. Gerspach
Purchased 65,000 shares @ $1.20

03/03/09
Roberto Hernandez
Purchased 6.0 million shares @ $1.25

52 week low price: $0.97
Closing Price (05/12/09): $3.87

SOURCE:
Moneycentral.msn.com
Insider Trading Transactions and Stock Quote
Date: 05/12/09

APPENDIX M

GENERAL ELECTRIC: INSIDER TRADING

03/03/09
Ralph Larsen
Purchased 30,000 shares @ $7.00

03/02/09
Jeffrey Immelt
Purchased 50,000 shares @ $8.89

03/02/09
Claudio Gonzalez
Purchased 20,000 shares @ 7.00

03/02/09
Samuel A. Nunn, Jr.
Purchased 30,000 shares @ $7.00

03/02/09
Michael Neal
Purchased 50,000 shares @ $7.90

03/03/09
Michael Neal
Purchased 25,000 shares @ $7.59

03/03/09
John Rice
Purchased 50,000 shares @ $7.04

03/03/09
Michael Neal
Purchased 25,000 shares @ $6.99
GLOSSARY of SELECTED TERMS

03/04/09
Michael Neal
Purchased 50,000 shares @ $7.05

52 week low price: $5.73
Closing Price (05/12/09): $13.68

Moneycentral.msn.com
Insider Trading Transactions and Stock Quote
Date: 05/12/09

Glossary of Selected Terms

Anarchy – a state of disorder due to lack of government or control.[552]

Cabal – a secret political clique or faction.[553]

Capitalism – an economic and political system in which a country's trade and industry are controlled by private owners for profit, rather than by the state.[554]

Civility, duty of – "In choosing a constitution, then, and in adopting some form of majority rule, the parties accept the risks of suffering the defects of one another's knowledge and sense of justice in order to gain the advantages of an effective legislative procedure. There is no other way to manage a democratic regime. ... The duty of civility imposes a due acceptance of the defects of institutions and a certain restraint in taking advantage of them. Without some recognition of thus duty mutual trust and confidence are liable to break down."[555]

Command System – is the opposite of a *market system*. An economy that allocates resources through the centralized decisions of the nation's central government. It is an economy associated with Marxist-Communism. See Market System.

Commodity Futures Trading Commission (CFTC) – The federal

---

[552] Pearsall, p. 47.
[553] Ibid, 193.
[554] Ibid, p. 207.
[555] Rawls, p. 355.

regulatory agency established by the CFTC Act of 1974 to administer the Commodity Exchange Act.[556]

Communism – a theory or system of social organization in which all property is vested in the community and each person contributes and receives according to their ability and needs. A theory derived from Marxism.[557]

Communist Manifesto – was written by Karl Marx and Friedrich Engels in 1847 and published in London in February 1848. Its primary purpose was to announce and publicize that the communists had given up on the conspiratorial activities of the past and were now entering the scene of politics through an open declaration of principle.[558]

Compact theory – a statement of political philosophy derived from the Revolution asserting the compact theory of the state and the limited character of federal sovereignty.[559]

Confederation – an alliance of a number of parties or groups. A more or less permanent union of states with some political power vested in a central authority.[560]

Conservative – averse to change or innovation and holding traditional values. In a political context, favoring free enterprise, private ownership and socially conservative ideas.[561]

Constitution – a body of fundamental principles or established precedents according to which a state or organization is governed.[562]

Corrupt – willing to act dishonestly in return for money or personal gain. Morally depraved.[563]

---

[556] CFTC *Glossary*, p. 13.
[557] Pearsall, p. 289
[558] Marx, p. xiii.
[559] Kelly, p. 134.
[560] Pearsall, p. 298.
[561] Ibid, p. 303.
[562] Ibid, p. 305.
[563] Ibid, p. 321.

Decadent – characterized by or reflecting a state of moral or culture decline.[564]

Deconstruct – analyze (a text, conceptual system, etc.) by deconstruction, dismantle and expose the workings of: *social forms will have to be deconstructed before socialism can develop.*[565]

Democracy – a form of government in which the people have a voice in the exercise of power, typically through elected representatives. Control of a group by the majority of its members.[566]

Derivative – (of a financial product) having a value deriving from an underlying variable asset. Finance (often **derivatives**) a derivative future, option, or other financial product.[567]

Dictator- a ruler with total power over a country. An autocratic person.[568]

Doctrine – a set of beliefs or principles held and taught by a Church, political party or other group.[569]

Dogma – a principle or set of principles laid down by an authority as incontrovertible.[570]

Dual federalism – In matters distinct from slavery the chief significance of dual federalism was to release state power for economic and social purposes. It remains briefly to consider the use that the states made of the power that developed upon them during the era of dual federalism.[571]

Duoism – is an emerging socioeconomic and political "ism" in America. It gained socio-political momentum in the early 1960s with the emergence

---

[564] Ibid, p. 370.
[565] Ibid, p. 373.
[566] Ibid, pp. 380-381.
[567] Ibid, p. 386.
[568] Ibid, p. 398.
[569] Ibid, p. 421.
[570] Ibid, p. 423.
[571] Kelly, p. 239.

of the New Left Movement. It gained economic momentum in the early 1980s during the Reagan Administration.

Duoism operates as de facto partnerships between large corporations, banks and the federal government. It is governed by elites who move back and forth through an archway between the federal government and industry.

Duoism's social model is *Marxist-Socialism*. Its Playbook is **The Communist Manifesto** *and* OTHER WRITINGS. Its economic paradigm is *Libertarianism*.

Duoism embraces lax rules and weak federal regulation of the nation's banking and manufacturing industries. This is the preferred method of government oversight. When regulation is required, it is written with ambiguity. Oligarchy elites attack their political opposition by drawing from *Nazi* and *Marxist* playbooks. They engage in character assassination and make *ad hominem* attacks on their opponents. The masses are controlled through the implementation of strict *politically correct* speech codes which is the required method of communication. Its form of governance is *Totalitarian*.

Egoism – an ethical theory that treats self-interest as the foundation of morality.[572]

Family – a group consisting of two parents and their children living together as a unit. A group of people related by blood or marriage. The children of a person or couple. All the descendants of a common ancestor.[573]

Fascism – an authoritarian and nationalistic (left-wing) system of government.[574]

Financial Accounting Standards Board (FASB) – since 1973, is the designated organization who establishes financial standards for accounting purposes in the preparation of financial reports by non-governmental entities.[575]

---

[572] Pearsall, p. 457.
[573] Ibid, p. 512.
[574] Ibid, p. 515.
[575] FASB Website.

Futures contract- An agreement to purchase or sell a commodity for delivery in the future: (1) at a price that is determined at initiation of the contract; (2) which obligates each party to the contract to fulfill the contract at the specified price; (3) which is used to assume or shift price risk; and (4) which may be satisfied by delivery or offset.[576]

GSifis – Global systemically important financial institutions. GSifis are twenty of the world's largest banks. Their failure would not be contained at home, but rather cause major ripples (contagion) on the international financial landscape

Hedging – Taking a position in a futures market opposite to a position held in the cash market to minimize the risk of financial loss from an adverse price change; a purchase or sale of futures as a temporary substitute for a cash transaction that will occur later.[577]

Ideologue – a dogmatic or uncompromising adherent of an ideology.[578]

Ideology – a system of ideas and ideals forming the basis of an economic or political theory.[579]

Keynesian – of or relating to the theories of the English economist John Maynard Keynes (1883-1946).[580]

Laissez-faire – a policy of non-interference, especially abstention by governments from interfering in the workings of the free market.[581]

Liberal – (in a political context) favouring individual liberty, free trade, and moderate political and social reform.[582]

Libertarianism – an extreme *laissez-faire* political philosophy advocating only minimal state intervention in the lives of citizens.[583]

---

[576] CFTC *Glossary*, p. 29.
[577] Ibid, p. 32.
[578] Pearsall, p. 705.
[579] Ibid.
[580] Ibid, p. 776.
[581] Ibid, p. 795.
[582] Ibid, p. 818.
[583] Ibid.

Liberty – the state of being free from oppression or imprisonment. The power or scope to act as one pleases. [584]

Mark-to-the-Market – Daily cash flow system used by U.S. futures exchanges to maintain a minimum level of margin equity for a given futures or option contract position by calculating the gain or loss in each contract position resulting from changes in the price of the futures or option contracts at the end of each trading day.[585]

Market System – an economy that allocates resources through the decentralized decisions of many firms and households as they interact in markets for goods and services.[586]

Marxism – the political and economic theories of Karl Marx and Friedrich Engels, later developed by their followers to form the basis for the theory and practice of communism.[587]

Muckraking – the action of searching out and publicizing scandal about famous people. A term coined by President Theodore Roosevelt in a speech (1906) alluding to Bunyan's *Pilgrim's Progress* and the man with the *muck rake*.[588]

Nazi – *historical* a member of the National Socialist German Workers' Party.[589]

Ochlocracy – government by the populace; mob rule.[590]

Oligarchy – a small group of people having control of a state. A state governed by such a group.[591]

Over-the-Counter (OTC) – in futures trading, a marketplace other than a CFTC designated contract market.

---

[584] Ibid.
[585] CFTC *Glossary*, p. 40.
[586] Mankiw, p. 836.
[587] Pearsall, p. 875.
[588] Ibid, p. 933.
[589] Ibid, p. 952.
[590] Ibid, p. 984.
[591] Ibid, p. 992.

Political correctness – the avoidance of forms of expression or action that are perceived to exclude, marginalize, or insult groups of people who are socially disadvantaged or discriminated against.

Progressive – A sociopolitical movement in America (1890-1920). Embraces conventional liberalism to include respectful and accepting of behavior or opinions different from one's own; open to new ideas. Favorable to individual rights and freedoms. Favoring social reform. Favoring change or innovation.[592]

Republic – a state in which supreme power is held by the people and their elected representatives, and which has an elected or nominated president rather than a monarch.[593]

Revolution – a forcible overthrow of a government or social order in favor of a new system. (In Marxism) the class struggle expected to lead to political change and the triumph of communism.[594]

Securities and Exchange Commission (SEC) – mission is to protect investors, maintain fair, orderly, and efficient markets, and facilitate capital formation.[595]

Separation theory – is the opposite of the theory of mixed government. Its objective is to achieve balance in government, or the theory of the separation of powers. The goal is to preserve liberty.[596]

Socialism – a political and economic theory of social organization which advocates that the means of production, distribution, and exchange should be owned or regulated by the community as a whole. (in Marxist theory) a transitional social state between the overthrow of capitalism and the realization of Communism.[597]

Speculator – In commodity futures, an individual who does not hedge, but

---

[592] Ibid, pp. 818 and 1142.
[593] Ibid, p. 1216.
[594] Ibid, p. 1226.
[595] SEC Website.
[596] Kelly, p. 71.
[597] Pearsall, p. 1362.

who trades with the objective of achieving profits through the successful anticipation of price movements.[598]

Swap – In general, the exchange of one asset or liability for a similar asset or liability for the purpose of lengthening or shortening maturities, or raising or lowering coupon rates, to maximize revenue or minimize financing costs. In securities, this may entail selling one issue and buying another; in foreign currency, it may entail buying a currency on the spot market and simultaneously selling it forward. Swaps may also involve exchanging income flows; for example, exchanging the fixed rate coupon stream of a bond for a variable rate payment stream; or vice versa, while not swapping the p[principal component of the bond.[599]

Totalitarianism – a distinctively modern form of dictatorship based not only on terror but also on mass support mobilized behind an ideology prescribing radical social change. It forms the minds of the population through control of all communications.[600]

Tyranny – cruel and oppressive government or rule. > a state under such rule. Cruel and arbitrary exercise of power or control. Rule by a tyrant.[601]

Union – a political unit consisting of a number of states or provinces with the same central government, especially the US or the UK.[602]

Welfare state – a system whereby the state undertakes to protect the health and well-being of its citizens, especially those is need, by means of grants, pensions, and other benefits.[603]

---

[598] CFTC *Glossary*, p. 56.
[599] Ibid, pp. 58-59.
[600] Craig, p. 1023.
[601] Pearsall, p. 1552.
[602] Ibid, p. 1567.
[603] Ibid, p. 1625.

BIBLIOGRAPHY

Abelson, Alan. Send in the Magicians. New York: *Barron's*. June 20, 2011.

Alighieri, Dante. *Inferno. Canto 14.* New York: Oxford University Press, 1996.

Alpert, Bill. Pickens' Clean Energy Stock Runs Out of Gas. *Barron's*. November 22, 2010.

Anderson, Fred. (ed.). *George Washington Remembers.* New York: Rowman & Littlefield Publishers, Inc., 2004.

Arendt, Hannah. *On Revolution.* New York: The Viking Press, 1963.

Arendt, Hannah. *The Origins of Totalitarianism.* New York: The World Publishing Company, 1958.

Arthur, Henry B. *Commodity Futures as a Business Management Tool.* Boston: Division of Research, Graduate School of Business, Harvard University, 1971.

Babiarz, Liz. Surgeons plan to close shop. Frederick: *Frederick News-Post.* November 2004.

Bailyn, Bernard. *Faces of Revolution.* New York: Vintage Books, 1992.

Bailyn, Bernard. *The Ideological Origins of the American Revolution.* Cambridge: The Belknap Press of Harvard University Press, 1992.

Bailyn, Bernard. *The Peopling of British North America*. New York: Vintage Books, 1986.

Barron's. April 13, 2009.

Bazelon, Emily. The Place of Women on the Court. New York: *The New York Times Magazine*, July 12, 2009.

Bentham, Jeremy. *An Introduction to the Principles of Morals and Legislation*. London: Oxford at the Clarendon Press, 1789.

Beier, Anne. *Crispus Attucks: Hero of the Boston Massacre*. New York: Rosen Publishing Group, 2003.

Boone, Peter and Johnson, Simon. The future of banking: is more regulation needed? London: *Financial Times*. Monday, April 11. 2011.

Bowling, Kenneth R. *The Founding Fathers and the Society of the Cincinnati*. Washington, DC: Symposium at the auditorium of The Phillips Collection, September 19, 2008.

Brands, H. W. *Andrew Jackson*. New York: Anchor Books, 2006.

Brickley, Adam. Government Takeover of GM 'Just Short of Socialism,' Economists Say. Washington: CNSNews.com. June 3, 2009.

Brigham, Eugene F. and Ehrhardt, Michael C. *Financial Management*. Mason: Thomson South-Western, 2008.

Bullock, Nicole. US munis face 'growing credit risk'. *Financial Times*. Wednesday, December 15, 2010.

Carlisle, Kristin. It's Like You're Walking But Your Feet Ain't Going Nowhere. Texas: National Housing Institute, Issue #147, Fall 2006.

Carlson, Tucker. Sued Sick. *Reader's Digest*. October 2002.

Carroll, Lewis. *Through the Looking-Glass and What Alice Found There*. New York: Barnes & Noble Classics, 2004.

Cavender, Nancy M. and Kahane, Howard. *Logic and Contemporary Rhetoric*. Belmont: Wadsworth, CENGAGE Learning, 2010.

Chernow, Ron. *Alexander Hamilton*. New York: Penguin Books, 2004.

Chaucer, Geoffrey. *The Canterbury Tales*. New York: Barnes & Noble Classics, 2006.

Churchill, Winston. Blood, Sweat and Tears. May 13, 1940.

Collier, Paul and Dollar, David. *Globalization, Growth and Poverty*. Washington, DC: The World Bank, 2002.

Cooke, Alistair. *Alistair Cooke's America*. New York: Alfred A. Knopf, Inc., 1973.

Craig, Edward. (ed.). *The Shorter Routledge Encyclopedia of Philosophy*. London: Taylor & Francis Group, 2005.

Croly, Herbert. *The Promise of American Life*. Boston: Northeaster University Press, 1989.

David Lean. *Doctor Zhivago*. DVD. Hollywood: MGM, 1965.

Economic Requirements Interpretative Statement: Policy Statement on Price Differentials. *U.S. Commodity Futures Trading Commission*. Washington, DC. May 31, 2010.

Edwards, Andrew. Inpiat Eskimos Jump Into PIPP. New York: *The Wall Street Journal*, August 10, 2009.

Eliot, T. S. *The Waste Land and Other Poems*. New York: Harcourt, Brace & World, Inc., 1934.

Figlewski, Stephen. How to Lose Money in Derivatives. The Journal of Derivatives. Winter 1994, Vol. 2, No. 2. New York: Institutional Investor, Inc., 1994.

Fischel, Daniel R. Regulatory Conflict and Entry Regulation of New Futures Contracts. The Journal of Business, Vol. 59, No. 2, pp. S85-S102, April, 1986.

Folsom, Burton. What's Wrong with the Progressive Income Tax? Midland: Mackinac Center for Public Policy, 1999.

Friedan, Betty. *The Feminine Mystique*. New York: W. W. Norton & Company, 1963.

Friedman, Milton. *Capitalism and Freedom*. Chicago: The University of Chicago Press, 1962.

Futures Industry Institute. *Guide to U.S. Futures Regulation*. Washington, DC: November 1995.

Galante, Joseph and Thomson, Amy. Government cutbacks rouse bleak forecast from Cisco Systems. *Washington Post*. Thursday, November 11, 2010.

Goldberg, Jonah. *Liberal* **FASCISM**. *The Secret History of the* AMERICAN LEFT *from* MUSSOLINI *to the* POLITICS OF MEANING. New York: Doubleday, 2007.

Gordon, John Steele. A Fiasco That Fed the Great Depression. New York: *Barron's,* December 15, 2008.

Gornick, Janet C. and Meyers, Marcia K. *Families That Work.* New York: Russell Sage Foundation, 2005.

Guerrera, Francesco, Baer, Justin and Braithwaite, Tom. Wall street set to sidestep 'Volcker rule'. *The Financial Times.* Thursday, November 11, 2010.

Haakonssen, Knud. (ed.). *The Law of Nations.* Indianapolis: Liberty Fund, Inc., 2008.

Hall, Kevin G. New Rules to Affect Valuation of Toxic Assets. San Diego: *The Union-Tribune,* April 2, 2009.

Hartung, William D. *Prophets of War:* Lockheed Martin and the Making of the Military-Industrial Complex. New York: Nation Books, 2011.

Harvard College *vs.* Armory, 9 Pick. (26 Mass.) 446, 461 (1830).

Hayward, Ph.D, Steven, F. The Role of Punitive Damages in Civil Litigation: New Evidence from Lawsuit Filings. *Pacific Research Institute.* 11/3/2010.

Hegel, Georg Wilhelm Friedrich. *The Philosophy of History.* New York: P. F. Collier & Son, 1900.

Hitler, Adolf. *Mein Kampf.* Boston: Houghton Mifflin Company, 1971.

Hobbes, Thomas. *Leviathan.* Cambridge: Cambridge University Press, 1991.

Hudson, David L. hate speech & campus speech codes. firstamendmentcenter.org.

Huntington, Samuel P. *Who Are We?* New York: Simon & Schuster, 2004.

Ishikawa, Tetsuya. *How I Caused the Credit Crunch.* London: Icon Books Ltd., 2009.

Jenkins, Patrick. Banks shift assets to cut pension deficits. *Financial Times.* Monday, August 22, 2011.

Kant, Immanuel. *Perpetual Peace and Other Essays.* Indianapolis: Hackett Publishing Company, 1983.

Kegley, Mary B. *Early Adventures on the Western Waters. Volume III, Part* 2. Marceline: Walsworth Publishing Company, 1995.

Kelly, Alfred H., Harbison, Winfred A. and Belz, Herman. *The American Constitution Its Origins and Development: Volume 1.* New York: W. W. Norton & Company, 1991.

Kelly-Gangi, Carol. (ed.). *Thomas Jefferson A Life.* New York: Harper Perennial, 1994.

Ketcham, Ralph. *James Madison a Biography.* Charlottesville: University of Virginia Press, 1990.

Ketcham, Ralph. (ed.). *The Anti-Federalist Papers and the Constitutional Convention Debates.* New York: Signet Classic, 2003.

Keynes, John Maynard. *The General Theory of Employment, Interest, and Money.* Amherst: Prometheus Books, 1997.

King's College London. International Center for Prison Studies. London: King's College London-School of Law, 2009.

Klein, Joe. America from the Road. *Time.* October 18, 2010.

Klein, Naomi. *No Logo.* New York: Picador, 2002.

Klein, Naomi. *The Shock Doctrine.* New York: Henry Holt & Company, 2007.

Letterman, David. *The Late Show.* New York: CBS, June 8, 2009.

Lewis, Sinclair. *Main Street.* New York: Barnes & Noble Classics, 2003.

Link, Arthur S. *Woodrow Wilson and the Progressive Era.* New York: Harper & Row, Publishers, Inc., 1954.

Locke, John. *The Second Treatise of Government and A Letter Concerning Toleration.* Mineola: Dover Publications, Inc., 2002.

Machiavelli, Niccolo. *Discourses on Livy.* Chicago: The University of Chicago Press, 1996.

Malkin, Michelle. *Culture of Corruption*. Washington, DC: Regnery Publishing, Inc., 2009.

Manhattan Institute for Policy Research. *Education Working Paper No. 3*. September 2003.

Mankiw, N. Gregory. *Principles of Economics*. Mason: Thomson South-Western, 2007.

Mapp, Jr., Alf J. *The Faiths of Our Fathers*. New York: Fall River Press, 2006.

Marcuse, Herbert. *One-Dimensional Man*. Boston: Beacon Press, 1964.

Marx, Karl and Engels, Friedrich. *The Communist Manifesto and Other Writings*. New York: Barnes & Noble Classics, 2005.

McCullough, David. *John Adams*. New York: Touchstone, 2002.

McTague, Jim. Last Word on the Crisis? New York: *Barron's*. January 31, 2011.

Meltzer, Allan H. *A History of the Federal Reserve. Volume 1: 1913-1951*. Chicago: The University of Chicago Press, 2003.

Michael Moore. *Capitalism: A Love Story*. DVD. Beverly Hills: Paramount Vantage, 2010.

Mill, John Stuart. *The Subjection of Women*. Mineola: Dover Publication, Inc., 1997.

Milton, John. *Paradise Lost*. Mineola: Dover Publications, Inc., 2005.

Morison, Samuel E., Commager, Henry S. and Leuchtenburg, William E. *A Concise History of the American Republic*. New York: Oxford University Press, 1983.

Moneycentral.msn.com. Bank of America Corp: Insider Trading. May 12, 2009.

Moneycentral.msn.com. Citigroup Inc: Insider Trading. May 12, 2009.

Moneycentral.msn.com. General Electric Co., Insider Trading. May 12, 2009.

Morgan, Edmund S. *Benjamin Franklin*. New Haven: Yale University Press, 2003.

Mussolini, Benito. *The Political and Social Doctrine of Fascism*. Mineola: Dover Publications, Inc., 1932.

Newman, Rick. <u>9 Signs of America's Decline</u>. *U.S. News and World Report*. October 26, 2009.

Nietzsche, Friedrich. *Beyond Good and Evil*. New York: Vintage Books, 1966.

Packard, Vance. *The Pyramid Climbers*. New York: McGraw-Hill Book Company, Inc., 1962.

Page, William Tyler. <u>The American's Creed</u>. Washington, DC: Accepted by the United States House of Representatives, April 13, 1918.

Paine, Thomas. *Common Sense and The Crisis*. Garden City: Anchor Books, 1973.

Parry, Jay A. and Allison, Andrew M. *The Real George Washington*. Malta: National Center for Constitutional Studies, 2009.

Paulson, Jr., Henry M. *On the Brink*. New York: Hachette Book Group, 2010.

Pearsall, Judy. (ed.). *The Concise Oxford Dictionary*. New York: Oxford University Press, 1999.

Peter, Laurence J. *Peter's Quotations.* New York: Bantam Books, 1977.

Pojman, Louis P. and Vaughn, Lewis. *Philosophy: The Quest for Truth.* New York: Oxford University Press, 2009.

Putnam, Robert D. *Bowling Alone.* New York: Simon & Schuster Paperbacks, 2000.

Randall, Willard Sterne. *Thomas Jefferson: A Life.* New York: Harper Perennial, 1994.

Rawls, John. *A Theory of Justice.* Cambridge: Harvard University Press, 1971.

Reilly, Frank K. and Brown, Keith C. *Investment Analysis and Portfolio Management.* Mason: Thomson South-Western, 2006.

Robert Wood Johnson Foundation.

Robertson, Ph.D., Diana C. <u>Business Ethics</u>. VHS Format. Philadelphia: *The Wharton School* of the University of Pennsylvania, 1988.

Roop, Connie and Peter. *The Diary of Joseph Plumb Martin, a Revolutionary War Soldier.* Tarrytown: Benchmark Books, 2001.

Rossiter, Clinton. (ed.). *The Federalist Papers.* New York: Signet Classic, 2003.

Rousseau, Jean-Jacques. *On the Social Contract.* Indianapolis: Hackett Publishing Company, 1987.

Schier, Steven E. *By Invitation Only.* Pittsburgh: University of Pittsburgh Press, 2000.

Schlesinger, Jr., Arthur M. *The Disuniting of America: Reflections on a Multicultural Society.* New York: W. W. Norton & Company, 1998.

Shilts, Richard. <u>Futures and Binary Options Based on Box Office Receipts</u>. Statement: CFTC, May 19, 2010.

Sinclair, Upton. *The Jungle*. New York: Barnes & Noble Classics, 2003.

Skousen, Ph.D., Mark. (ed.). *The Compleated Autobiography by Benjamin Franklin*. Washington, DC: Regnery Publishing, Inc., 2007.

Smith, Adam. *The Wealth of Nations*. New York: The Modern Library, 2000.

Smith, Ron. <u>Fort Hood massacre shows how political correctness can kill</u>. *The Baltimore Sun*. Friday, November 13, 2009.

Sorkin, Andrew Ross. *Too Big to Fail*. New York: Viking, 2009.

Soros, George. <u>Better to rescue banks than states</u>. *Financial Times*. Wednesday, December 15, 2010.

Soros, George. *The Crash of 2008 and What It Means*. New York: Public Affairs, 2008.

Sugrue, Ph.D., Michael. Princeton University. <u>Lecture Twelve: The Frankfurt School</u>. Springfield: *The Teaching Company*, 1995.

Sun Tzu. *The Art of War*. London: Shambhala Publications, Inc., 1991.

Taylor, Alan. *American Colonies*. New York: Penguin Books, 2001.

Taylor, Timothy. Macalester College. <u>Lecture Seven: The Economy for the Soviet Union.</u> Chantilly: *The Teaching Company*, 2008.

The Avalon Project. *Thomas Jefferson's First Inaugural Address*. New Haven: Yale Law School, June 19, 2009.

The Avalon Project. *Washington's Farewell Address 1796*. New Haven: Law Law School, April 10, 2009.

The CONSTITUTION *of the* United States.

The Economist. A new sheriff. Washington, DC: September 5th-11th 2009.

The New York Times. How Bright Promise in Cancer testing Fell Apart. Friday, July 8, 2011.

The New York Times. MF Global's Shortfall No Surprise, Some Say. Wednesday, March 28, 2012.

The New York Times. Paterson Asks Ethics Panel to Quit After Report Finds Leaks in Spitzer Inquiry. Thursday, May 14, 2009.

The New York Times. Tea Party Focus Turns to Senate And Shake-up. Sunday, May 13, 2012.

The Wall Street Journal. Challenges in Chasing Fraud. June 23, 2011.

The Wall Street Journal. Congress Helped Banks Defang Key Rule. June 3, 2009.

The Wall Street Journal. Growing Criticism at Home Took Toll on Palin. July 6, 2009.

The Wall Street Journal. Inupiat Eskimos Jump Into PPIP. August 10, 2009.

The Washington Post. The Regulatory Rift That Altered the Debate. October 15, 2008.

Triana, Pablo. Flawed Basel III could boost toxic leverage. *The Financial Times.* Monday, November 1, 2010.

Tucker, Robert C. *The Marx-Engels Reader.* New York: W. W. Norton & Company, 1978.

Unger, Harlow Giles. *The Last Founding Father.* Philadelphia: Da Capo Press, 2009.

USA Today. <u>For Boomers, Recession Is Redefining Retirement</u>. June 17, 2009.

U.S. Commodity Futures Trading Commission. *Glossary.* Washington, DC: CFTC Publications, 1992.

Whyte, Jr., William H. *The Organization Man.* Garden City: Doubleday Anchor Books, 1956.

www.abanet.org

www.americanhistorytimelines.com

www.bis.org/statistics/derstats.htm

www.blessedcause.org

www.cdc.gov. Advance Data. Number 323, May31, 2001.

www.census.gov. Table 83 on p. 4 of Section 2. 2003 Statistical Abstract.

www.examiner.com. 1/21/2010.

www.familyfirstaid.org. May 25, 2009.

www.forthepeople.com. October 31, 2010.

www.gallup.com/poll/120857. June 27, 2009.

www.gene.com

www.Huffingtonpost.com

www.independentvoting.org.

www.informingvoters.org.

www.nationalatlas.gov.

www.ncrc.rutgers.edu.

www.orthodoxytoday.org. 1/21/2010.

www.sterlingtimes.com.

www.thefire.org

www.theKingcenter.org.

www.usdoj.gov. August 4, 2009.

www.worldbank.org. August 4, 2009.

Yao, Yang and Yueh, Linda. *Globalisation and Economic Growth in China.* London: World Scientific Publishing Co., 2006.

Young, Alfred F. *Masquerade.* New York: Vintage Books, 2004.

Zagarri, Rosemarie. (ed.). David Humphreys' *"Life of General Washington."* Athens: University of Georgia Press, 1991.

Zuniga, Marielena. Is There a Doctor in the House? *Best for Women.* March/April/May 2008.

INDEX